African Voices

African Voices

Selected by Howard Sergeant, 1914-

Lawrence Hill and Company

New York · Westport

Selection and introduction,
© Howard Sergeant 1973

All Rights Reserved. No part of this
publication may be reproduced, stored in a
retrieval system, or transmitted in any form
or by any means, electronic, mechanical,
photocopying, recording or otherwise, without
prior permission.

Published in the United States by permission
of Evans Brothers Limited, London.

Lawrence Hill & Co. Publishers, Inc., September 1973

ISBN 0-88208-016-4

Printed in Great Britain

Contents

Acknowledgements

For permission to use copyright poems, the editor and the publishers are indebted to the authors concerned and to the following:

East African Publishing House for 'My Name Blew Like a Horn Among the Payira' and 'The Graceful Giraffe Cannot Become a Monkey' by Okot p'Bitek from *Song of Lawino*;

Mrs Jean Farrant for 'Naming the Child' and 'African Dancing' by Eric Mazani;

Heinemann Educational Books Ltd for 'Above Us, Only Sky' and 'Our Aims Our Dreams Our Destinations' by Dennis Brutus from *Letters to Martha*, and 'Letter to Mamma' by I. Choonara from *Seven South African Poets*;

David Higham Associates for 'Words of Wisdom and Love' by Abioseh Nicol;

Longman Group Ltd for 'A Sandal on the Head' by Kwesi Brew from *The Shadows of Laughter*, and 'Our History' by Mbella Sonne Dipoko from *West African Verse*;

Mbari Publications for 'Sirens, Knuckles, Boots' by Dennis Brutus from *Sirens, Knuckles, Boots*.

Acknowledgements are due to the following publications which first printed the poems indicated:

African Arts/Arts d'Afrique: 'A Lament for my Step-mother Country' by I. Choonara;

Black Orpheus: 'Look into a Mirror' by Romanus N. Egudu, 'Is it True?' and 'Fugue for Power' by Aigboje Higo, 'Elegy of the Wind' by Christopher Okigbo and 'Voices', 'For Her' and 'Night Encounter' by Ken Tsaro-Wiwa;

Busara: 'Queens' by Benedict Oguto;

Chirimo: 'Tell Me The Reason' by N. S. Sigogo;

Drum Beat: 'Child Growing So Big' by Walter Bgoya, 'Walking Backwards' by John Mbiti and 'Rain Breaking on Roof Thatch' by Edwin Waiyaki;

Outposts: 'A Sandal on the Head' by Kwesi Brew;

Transition: 'Flight/The Exile/Exit' by Dennis Brutus;

Two Tone: 'To My Elders', 'The Sun Goes Up and Up' and 'Praying for New Life' by Henry Pote;
Zuka: 'June 1967' by Amin Kassam, 'Christmas 1967' by David Rubadiri and 'The Rupture' by Edwin Waiyaki.

For kind assistance and advice the editor wishes to express special thanks to: Lionel Abrahams, N. K. Adzakey of Ghana Universities Press, Margaret Amoso, Medical Librarian at Ibadan University, Jared Angira, Dr Jawa Apronti, Dennis Brutus, Adam Butcher of the Oxford University Press in Nigeria, Professor F. G. Butler, Mrs N. H. Buttress, Dr Angus Calder, Professor F. C. A. Cammaerts, Cyprian Ekwensi, Peggy Harper, Ime Ikiddeh, Jonathan Kariara, Amin Kassam, Cathy Oswald of the Africa Division of Longman Group Ltd, Keith Sambrook of Heinemann Educational Books Ltd, Dr J. E. Stewart, Efua T. Sutherland and O-lan Style.

Whilst every effort has been made to trace the owners of copyright, in a few cases this has proved impossible, and we take this opportunity of tendering our apologies to any authors whose rights may have been unwittingly infringed. In particular, we would like to hear from Khadambi Asalache, Walter Bgoya, Mbella Sonne Dipoko, Romanus N. Egudu, Richard Rive and Edwin Waiyaki.

Introduction

As I have pointed out in various books and articles, there has been something resembling a cultural upheaval in Africa during the last ten years or more, so that one might be justified in maintaining that Africa is beginning to emerge as a new and dynamic force, adding a freshness and perhaps even a new dimension to the English language. Some of the most interesting and exciting poetry written in English at the present time is coming from Africa, and it is hoped that this collection of recent poetry by African poets will give readers some idea of the cultural developments taking place on the African continent today.

In presenting this anthology, however, I do not claim to have included the work of every poet of merit—indeed, for such a representation to have been at all possible, it would have been necessary to double the size of the volume. For instance, I have been unable to secure recent poems from Kofi Awoonor, Taban Lo Liyong, Ezekiel Mphahlele, Cosmo Pieterse, Lewis Nkosi, Michael Echeruo and Efua Sutherland in time for this collection; and there are at least thirty other poets whose work might have been included if space had allowed. White Africans have not been represented here, firstly because their work, having been widely published in the English-speaking countries, is already well-known and it seemed more sensible to devote the available space to the work of poets unknown outside Africa; and secondly, because the experience of white African poets, owing much to European traditions and cultural heritage, has inevitably been different from that of non-white Africans. Similarly, limitation of space has prevented the inclusion of translations either from the great African vernaculars or the work of African poets who use French as their vehicle of expression. Perhaps I should also mention that the space allocated to each poet in this collection should not be regarded as an attempt to measure relative stature in any way, for I have deliberately given more space to new and little-known poets than to such well-established poets as Wole Soyinka, John Pepper Clark, and Gabriel Okara.

Since so many European critics, though accustomed to the diversities of, say, English, French, Italian and German literatures, are inclined to discuss 'African literature' as if it were the product of a single culture, I would like to make it clear—to European and American readers—that the African poets whose work is included in this anthology represent a wide variety of cultures. What is even more important is that, though they are Nigerians, Ghanaians, Kenyans, Ugandans, or Tanzanians, etc., they write as individuals, concerned with the communication of a particular experience. It is for this reason that I have presented the poets in alphabetical order, regardless of nationality, instead of grouping them as Nigerians, Ugandans, etc.

In the Introduction to my *Commonwealth Poems of Today*, published in 1967, I observed: 'So far as the countries which have achieved self-government since the war are concerned, it is too early to look for distinguishing characteristics or dominant trends in the poetry written in English, though some of these countries have made considerable progress in an incredibly short time. Perhaps the only thing that can be said with any degree of certainty is that whatever poetic traditions emerge will reflect the historical, racial and social patterns of the different nations, and that the individual poets will develop the forms of expression most appropriate to their needs.'

Since this is a kind of interim report (for it is still too early to make pronouncements), readers may wish to know what developments, if any, can be discerned. Are the emerging traditions beginning to reflect the historical, racial and social patterns of this troubled continent?

Certainly the problem of language is still a dominant one, and it will no doubt continue to be, though the African poets seem to be tackling it in a realistic and effective manner. If the African poet chooses to write his poems in English or French, rather than Yoruba, Hausa, Swahili or whatever his own language happens to be, he will certainly reach a wider audience, but at the same time he must—if he is to be authentic—use this second language to explore the African experience and guard against taking over ideas and attitudes alien to that experience. As we shall see in this anthology, there are different ways of dealing with the problem. The Ugandan poet, Okot p'Bitek, for instance, seems to be following the example set by the Nigerian poet, Gabriel Okara, by writing his *Song of Lawino* in his own language first and translating the results into English:

> Listen,
> My father comes from Payira,
> My mother is a woman of Koc!
> I am a true Acoli
> I am not a half-caste
> I am not a slave-girl;
> My father was not brought home
> By the spear
> My mother was not exchanged
> For a basket of millet.

Kwesi Brew, on the other hand, draws strongly upon the African way of life, making use of Ghanaian folk song and customs, whilst presenting the conflict between tribal instincts and habits, and modern national aspirations. His 'Consulting a Fetish' and 'The Market-Place in the North' illustrate the method, but 'A Sandal on the Head' is a significant development—the title of the poem is derived from the Ghanaian custom of touching the chief's head with one of his own sandals to declare him deposed, and the poem itself actually refers to the downfall of President Nkrumah in these traditional terms.

Whilst there are still poets protesting somewhat bitterly against the indignities which white societies have heaped upon the black peoples in the past (and this is very understandable), 'negritude' seems to have lost its appeal and, indeed, its force (though the concept always had more relevance for the French-speaking African states). What is distinctly noticeable, and perhaps to be expected, is that more and more African poets are rejecting the provocative slogans and the glib platitudes about the 'African self' and the 'African personality' in order to examine their own societies with greater critical awareness; and as a result more satire is being produced. More attention is being given to African history, African customs and landscape, though not in any spirit of adulation—indeed, one might argue that there is a new sense of social responsibility in evidence. Aigboje Higo, for instance, concludes his poem 'Is It True?' with the comment that 'This nation runs a multi-storey conscience', using a modern image with telling effect. Certainly, the poets are not afraid to laugh at themselves or ridicule the pretensions of their own politicians. In 'Question' Dr Jawa Apronti asks:

> Black Man,
> Won't you go to the Moon?
> Don't tell me the technology
> Of your juju
> Is unequal to the task.

and in 'You Talk to Me of "Self" ' Lenrie Peters throws a more realistic light upon the over-publicised and over-sentimental-ised notion of the 'African self':

> Octogenarian breasts at twenty
> enthroned in pools of urine
> after childbirth, whose future
> is not theirs to mould or flirt with mirth.

> There is your 'Self' crushed
> between the grinding wheel
> of ignorance and the centuries,
> the blood congealed in the baking sun

whilst in 'Resurrection', I. Choonara, able to rise above personal bitterness and anguish, finds hope for the multi-racial society of the future in what he sees of ordinary human love and compassion in the present:

> I saw a black child.
> Nose dripping, disgustingly, helplessly:
> White mucous, globular above the lip.
> Sultry, salty taste of childhood memories.
> I saw the black head, resting, nesting
> Beneath the bosom of a white woman,
> Grey-haired, love and tenderness
> For a child fostered upon her . . .

Kojo Gyinaye Kyei goes so far as to suggest to his countrymen that they should not criticise other people ('ruthless guests') for their troubles, but consider their own shortcomings, and even makes fun of racial intolerance in his 'Common Six Feet of Ground':

> Briton or Chinese,
> They all sneeze in loud or soft
> Whiiizzzimmmm buuummmms!
> One difference is that
> While the British are fantastic
> In *abinkyi* calculations
> With knives and forks,
> The Chinese can really swing
> On the jitterbug of chopsticks.

The poets are becoming increasingly confident in their own powers of expression and their choice of subject. Throughout this collection there is reflected an awareness of life outside Africa—and this in itself raises questions of the type to be found in Samson Amali's 'Our World and the Moon' and Ime Ikiddeh's 'Martin Luther King'—as well as a deep concern for Africa and the urgent need for Africans to work out their own destiny. Several poems in the anthology refer to the Nigerian Civil War, in which Christopher Okigbo lost his life, but it is John Pepper Clark who in 'The Casualties' attempts to write of war within the wider human context:

We fall,
All casualties of the war,
Because we cannot hear each other speak,
Because eyes have ceased to see the face from the crowd,
Because whether we know or
Do not know the extent of wrong on all sides,
We are characters now other than before
The war began, the stay-at-home unsettled
By taxes and rumours, the looters for office
And wares, fearful every day the owners may return,
We are all casualties . . .

Howard Sergeant

Samson O. O. Amali

Born in the ancient town of Upu, the traditional home of both the Oturkpo and the Oglewu people of Idoma Division, Benue-Plateau State of Nigeria, about 1946, Samson O. O. Amali attended the Methodist village school for four years, and then went to live with his aunt in Lagos. Since then he has lived in either Lagos or Ibadan, but he has visited his home frequently. He read English for his degree at the University of Ibadan. He writes his poems both in English and Idoma. He has written plays and articles, and his poems have appeared in *Black Orpheus*. A collection of his *Poems* (University Bookshop Nigeria Ltd) was published in 1968.

Our World and the Moon

(On seeing the first photograph of our crescent world from the moon. August 1966)

Two children
  A girl and a boy
Stand near me still
  Looking at me wondering
I sit still
  With the American first picture of our own world
    Taken from the moon's surface
    Showing clearly the crescent, white, cloudy world
  In my hand,
Lost in imagination of the distance of our world
  From the moon
The huge space between our world
  And the moon.

Still looking, leaning forward and peeping
  Into our world from the moon
My heart beats,

Aches
And ponders calmly, solemnly
And in a painful ecstasy and confusion
   It mutters:
'This is our world.
Oh, it sends out no roots
   Anywhere!
It is a small world
It's a shallow world
It's you and I
   Who make this world deep.'

I turn to the children.
They say nothing
I say nothing
They just stare calmly
   Guessing into my thoughts,
     Perhaps.
They do not know now.
Perhaps when they are grown
This world and the moon
   Will be near by
     For them.

Will it be man's universe?
   Perhaps.
And will man still be man?

Strides

Look at that child,
   trotting after his mother.
Her strides get wider and wider,
   faster and faster, unaware.
He quickens his trotting to catch up with her;
The more he tries
The more gap she leaves behind her for him.

Life contains both her and him.
Both share life, take out of life their own share,
   give to life what they have.

She strides on gracefully for her child and
    herself, unaware
Her child still follows her.

They shall never level
And even if they level
They will never be the same,
For life and nature have separated them eternally;
One contains the other
And each will remain a distinct self,
A mother and her child.

God

The beginning of the concept of God
    Acted and still acts as a focal point,
Where ideas, diverse ideas, converge,
    Where societies, diverse societies, converge,
To concentrate upon, to discuss in an intense way,
    In a brief time or for a long time,
To resolve in a peaceful and humble way
    Their common problems and human problems
        Creatively:
One of the mainsprings for delving
    Into human depths
    And into the world
    And human imagination and conceptions.

The beginning of the concept of God
    Is one of the beginnings of man's deep discovery
        of human dignity,
    Examination of himself and inner self;
    Of people, society, and things;
    Of his cool and quiet realisation
    Of his lonely self,
    And his lone existence
    In a cold and lonely world;
    Of his need to have a partner—
    An inseparable, near, invisible, far, and
        infinite partner—

To keep him alert,
Warm, compassionate, understanding,
Sympathetic, kind, secure.

But
God as a focal point likewise
Concentrates, reflects and emanates,
   Hatred, wickedness,
Destructive imaginings, plans, and actions
To make bombs, guns, arrows and poisons,
   For the killing of man
   And for the enslaving of man.

God and Man

Man trusts man very little
Because man is not always sure of man;
He may trust in God, what he could never see,
   what exists in his mind, and
   functions through motion, air
In man: this, man believes in and may die for,
   because he may never see it.
He may feel it, think of it, dream about
   and act for it;
He believes that this force is in him—
   his inner-heart is greater than himself.
He thinks it travels everywhere in him,
   and imagines it is everywhere.
This feeling in man, of a being higher than himself,
This feeling which exists in man's heart
Puts a check on man's excesses; it
   increases man's excesses, too.

Once a man has lived for a few seconds and dies,
He has left himself behind for the living,
Because he is a man, he shares the air with man,
He is born through man and dies like man, without air.
The dead child pulled from its mother's womb has
   affected man because it is man.
Although it cannot speak, act or breathe air,
   it is still man.

4

The only thing that differentiates it from the
    living child is that it does not breathe air,
    it can't breathe:
It is dead.

The air in man affects man,
    through man's feelings, actions and words;
Even death cannot destroy man's impact upon man,
    whether dead or alive, man knows that man is man.
The dead man leaves his image in the living,
    in his children and in other people.

It's noble for man to have a flexible mind
    that breathes, that can change and can't change,
    can move and can't move.
It's noble for man to look up to something in himself,
    to have something in him, which he thinks is
    higher than himself.
This gives him security, peace of mind and direction.
It gives him restlessness, too.
It makes him gregarious with himself.

Each man is a product of one system,
    embodies the system's apparatus.
There are variations, but they still make us all man.
Some man's apparatus may work differently from
    the others.

Man's physical and outward forms
Seem to depend upon the inner-form;
The inner-forms seem to depend upon the outward forms;
Both his soul—his inner-heart air, and his
    physical outward forms, function together,
    carry each other, depend on one thing—air;
They function separately at a point,
Are a part of each other.

The soul, because we can't see it,
    Because it is invisible and made up of air, lasts
        longer than
    The physical form of man.
The physical form of man dies and decays.

Air may never die. Man dies.
His air and image go off into the world and the universe
And into the living man;
Because we have souls in air, in us,
We take and combine with ours, the soul of the dead
    which is now also air in motion.

They move on always, from time to time.
His image is air that you and he have shared
    before he dies;
His image is his physical body, the things that he does and says
    before he dies.
Man is gregarious and infectious:
Man cannot leave man alone,
Because all men share and have many qualities
    in common.
They breathe and so live: they die.
They think, imagine and act—all between man and man
And within man. Fundamentally, they all have the
    same life, the same inner-hearts,
    whose functions depend upon nature,
    place, time and action of man.

Jared Angira

Born in 1947 on the Kenyan shore of Lake Victoria. He edited the literary magazine, *Busara*, when he was at the University College of Nairobi. His first book of poems, *Juices*, was published by the East African Publishing House.

On the Walls of Crossbars

The bay is dark, mother,
and you keep whispering.
The salt-laden air
dries my mouth
like a pregnant woman
the pebbles have frozen
with my scaly feet

hyenas howl
on my jelly-like courage
I have no bravery
I have no determination
I have no destination
My Mission is Survival
the mission of humanity

Now, mother
Why let your arms
dismember the pattern
passed to me
by the Celestial Beings?
Why dismantle
the Mono Concord
. . . beyond rebirth

When your love
descended upon my self
it failed to coil itself
in one chamber

there were many chambers
of the selves
who failed to agree
on the equal division
of this love
the hawks snatched it
the sun dried it
rain beat it
the skin was stretched
the skeletons,
lurid,
haunted the gatekeepers

Only under your wings
can son of man
get shelter
and why disown your feathers
and cut the twigs?
Without a nest
we admire the beauty of the butterfly.
Only none recalls
its emergence

    from the caterpillar
    The hairy centipede
    of legs unwanted
    stage of existence
    in the black labyrinth

O Mother
the patient
from malaria thirst
begs for water
Vomits the biliverdine.
Who will pass the tumbler

    to the cracked throat?
    The cracked throat
    like a cracked wall
    of an abandoned hut
    blood streams
    like rain
    through a dripping roof

Wasps
have built homes
on the future
leaving untouched
the bold-faced memory

opening the diary
coming across events
that sent memory mourning
behind the burial ground
I empty the dustbin
the street-sweeper
sweeps the bitter memory
to my father's tomb

Why watch me wriggle
O Mother
in the yellow marsh
of confusion?

Frustration comes
mounts my horse
to the battlefield
the front-line is hot
the horse is wounded
the soldier is lame.

He shall come to judge
the Quick and the Dead
death shall be quick
silence shall be quiet
existence shall be cold
like the sea-washed pebble.

May not the bull be warned
of the approaching castration?
Surviving generation
life being made for man
burn and turn not into ash
weep and shed not tears
fill the mouth with scum
and spit it not

eat grass and chew no cud
kneel on murram pavement
and walk on knees
but watch not the blood.

Mother, so poets must stand
at water's edge
and watch the ducks
swim across—
sea waves
mock humanity
that can never cross
the sea of misery
to the bank of happiness

abortive intercourse
in Time's bedroom—
search for conception
of joy and laughter
with one colour
the rainbow had left in a hurry

O Mother you yawn so much like all is on the Verge!

Lacrimae Prophetii

Pilgrims whose
bones have dissolved
from limbs
come trudging
recollections ignited
by a lone palm tree
near the oasis

they polluted
the drinking water
killed the fish
in that pond

they treated Time with respect
like a woman
underestimated her power
till she pushed them
in the dark railway compartment

courage creaks
like ungreased wagon wheel
the sinews lie prostrate
paralysed in the lapse
the marrow is blue

they obstructed the firemen
and watched buildings blaze
nature laughed to the bloodful teeth
and they obstructed the police
robbed banks of failures
the insurance house of success
mirrored under guard

after all the distant miles
they came to the quiet city
the mosque ashes puff silently
house razed to the ground
expectations are but distant cousins
of the cowpeas
reality in the whirling water-trough

Jawa Apronti

Born in 1940 at Keta, Ghana, Dr Jawa Apronti was educated at the Universities of Ghana, Leeds and London, and he is at present a Research Fellow in Linguistics at the Institute of African Studies, University of Ghana. He is married, with three children. His poems have appeared in various magazines, and he is co-editor of *Okyeame*, Ghana's literary magazine.

Question

Black Man,
Won't you go to the Moon?
Don't tell me the technology
Of your juju
Is unequal to the task.

It has caused rain
Outside the rainy season;
It has spoken
To our dead
In the words of the living.
Black Man,
Won't you go to the Moon?

You have watched silently,
As the others built ships
That carried you
To the land of the chain-gang.

You have looked on
In amazement
While lesser powers
Have conjured up
The iron horse,
The mammy wagon,
And the shining bird.

You sat there
While baked men
Took to the skies
In their shining houses.
Black Man,
Won't you go to the Moon?

This is the year of the Moon.
The chain-gang built
The Americans
And, this year,
They are going to the Moon.

Pluck your herb,
Chant your incantation,
Rattle your cowries,
Beat your drums,
Blow your horn
And take the lead
—As I think you can—
To the Moon.

Or,
Black Man,
Can't you go to the Moon?

Khadambi Asalache

Born in Tiriki, Western Kenya, in 1934. While studying Architecture at a Nairobi college, Khadambi Asalache assisted in establishing the nucleus of the student movement in Kenya and later, as Vice-President, secured its recognition in international student circles at a conference held in Tunis in 1959. His poems have appeared in many periodicals and he was represented in *Commonwealth Poems of Today* (Murray) and *New Voices of the Commonwealth* (Evans).

Fencesitters

They come on the screen of one's mind
Inverted, letters coming in succession; titles
Cancelled yet illuminated. Their words glide
On transparent wings. They are angels of flattery
Who rise and fall with the speed of mercury
And return into the bulb when the weather is cold.

They walk on pads in a dry season;
They colour and discolour themselves when a storm
Uproots tottering totems of heroes
Thrown into darkness. Later you find them in form
Climbing up hills, proclaiming aloud
'We've done it again, stopped the terrible catastrophe.'

Fencesitters are fish on a wrack of sand;
Chameleons wearing weatherproof suits, made to measure;
A false alarm permanently on guard
Unaware of a hidden monster, a caterpillar
Camouflaged in a shell, growing slowly
As it eats the roots of the shaky fence.

Wonder Banda

Wonder Maxwell Banda was born at Chikurubi, Rhodesia, in 1948. Educated at Highfield Secondary School, Fletcher High School and University College, Rhodesia. Hopes to become a journalist.

Thinking Red

Fifteen little red fish
Six red tomatoes
Cellar red pepper
Big red fire
And forty-five mouths.

I think of men as one man
With a full head and empty stomach,
One big tome under the left arm
Like a law student at varsity:
Red herrings at lectures, with prospects
Of red salmon in residence refectory.

They say Communists are red, too.
Royal colour.
Piri-piri chicken the colour of Communism
Is aggressive, too—tastewise.

Hey you!
Toi, au veston rouge!

c

Mao's army
Death
Hell-fire
Blood
Salvation?

He said the blood of Jesus. . . .
Today they'd call Him a red.

Save us from society
Save us from sin
From red thoughts
From boredom

Gaston Bart-Williams

Born in Sierra Leone in 1938. His works include *A Bouquet of Carnations* (BBC play), *The Lion Mountains* (BBC feature), *Science and Modern Africa* (BBC serial), and he has contributed to C.B.C. (Canada), Sveriges Radio (Sweden), N.R.K. (Norway), and W.D.R. (Germany). His work has been published in various magazines, including *Outposts* and *The London Magazine*. He has won a number of prizes, among them the All Africa Short Story Award and the Michael Karolyi International Award. He contributed to *Commonwealth Poems of Today* (Murray) and *New Voices of the Commonwealth* (Evans), and was one of the four poets selected by Howard Sergeant for his *Poetry from Africa* (Pergamon Press).

Read the Tea Leaves

again
my hand did not conceal it
I let the teapot drop
it is the inconsequential that counts
the broken porcelain
the tremor at the fingertips
the rattle in the head

NOTE THE INVENTORY

the silent bed
an empty teacup
old love letters
ten nervy fingers
broken porcelain

read the tea leaves

Voices from the Basement

      voices from the garret command
      voices from the basement threaten

present is the time
when our spirituals transcend
out of the basement
out of the ghettoes
out of the cities
out of the reins of commerce
into the spirit of the revolution
when our churches
museums of antiquity
institutions of antiquated modernity
transform into nerve centres
where the blood of the revolution
pulsates
present is the vibrant drum
that hammers out the eternal cry
for freedom

      voices from the garret command
      voices from the basement threaten

present is the dialectic drum
that takes ecclesiastical rites to court

      voices from the garret command
      voices from the basement threaten

out of the basement churches
is liberated the revolutionary God

      voices from the garret command
      voices from the basement threaten

I saw someone down the basement the other day
exchange the cross at the altar for a gun
I saw the other one
lay down his priestly habits
for army clothing

he took up jungle outfits
he entered guerilla service

    voices from the garret command
    voices from the basement threaten

I saw another one prepare
to destructuralise
the building
in order
to liberate himself
in order
to liberate the building itself
in order to liberate us

    voices from the garret command
    voices from the basement threaten

voices from the basement
will destructuralise
suppression
will destructuralise
abstractions
will destructuralise the bourgeois conception
of art and beauty
will destructuralise aesthetic and material norm
in order to liberate them
in order to liberate themselves
in order to liberate us all

    voices from the garret command
    voices from the basement threaten

voices from the basement
will materialise
into
concretefists
concretepunches
concretetruths
voices from the basement
will rise up to the garret
will spoil your garret-rest

voices from the basement
will give you indigestion when you eat
voices from the basement
will displace you from your seat
will destructuralise the building
will liberate themselves
will liberate you

voices from the garret command
voices from the basement threaten

Walter Bgoya

Born in Ngora in the West Lake District of Tanzania in 1931, Walter Bgoya was educated locally and at the University of Kansas, USA, where he graduated in International Relations and Economics. He is at present with the Ministry of Foreign Affairs in Dar es Salaam.

Child Growing So Big

Child growing so big
Weighing heavily on your mama's back,
Kicking your stocky feet
Carelessly on your mama's tursh,
Child boy in buck skin
Firmly pressing mama's breasts.

Child boy with kinky hair
  terraces on your round head,
What will you grow to be like
  off your mama's back,
Off the grass mattress
Away from the bleating goats by the river?

Will you grow to be like me
  lost in sky-scratching brick,
Or the soldier that your father was
Defending the sheep from the wolves,
Fighting for his lord's land,
Fighting for your mother's love?

Where is your father now,
Stocky legs innocent and young?

Where has he gone?

Your mother's eyes—their tired reclination;
Where's he gone, that half-schooled vagabond
Who left his goats—and your mother
To fight his other lords
As if he knew why?

Whatever you grow to be,
Be unlike him,
See the wolves clearly,
Leave, too, and go
But for me, brother baby,
Let me fight the sky creeping,
The pride furnaces firing guns far away,
The arrogance of God's favour; this that has
Left me sordid
In spite of myself;
Child brother grow;
I'll help—only help.

Kwesi Brew

Kwesi Brew was born in Ghana in 1928, a member of a Fante family which has played a distinguished part in Ghana's history. He was one of the first undergraduates at the University College of the Gold Coast (now the University of Ghana), where he was awarded a British Council poetry prize. He joined the Administrative Service of his country in 1953 and after Ghana achieved independence was transferred to the Foreign Service. He has since served as Ambassador for Ghana in England, France, India, Germany, USSR and Mexico, and is at present serving in Senegal. He was one of the four African poets featured in *Poetry from Africa* (Pergamon Press), edited by Howard Sergeant, and has since published his first volume of poems, *The Shadows of Laughter* (Longman).

Consulting a Fetish

They came. Sat down. Looked at its face
Cleft and cracked by the sun,
Its eyes were carved on short stilts
And there was a hollow where the balls should go;
Its lips were burnt black with holding
Back secrets it shared with those who never
    came back home.

Someone had told them it talked
    and told fortunes and
    revived lost causes.
They have been in its grove
    for three days and more,
Looking up expectantly at the burnt lips
    and hearing not a word.
So they can break their vigil and their fast
And go to tell the tale to a sad and weary people.

The Market-Place in the North

Out in the sun amid the reds
And greens of peppers and tomatoes
Were the lovely Konkomba boys,
Strong and straight as the teak;
   lovely boys,
Carrying their bows on
   a slender shoulder
And poisoned arrows in
   leather scabbards.
They had come to buy pito and
   to show their bodies
To the bare-bosomed girls
   of Navrongo.

It's all calm and quiet
   nowadays in the market-place.
The boys don't come any more.
But the girls still go there
   to look for them,
Holding a flimsy hope
   to their hearts
And a tear in their eyes.

Wooden Dolls and Dreams

While the drummers
Drummed
And the women
Danced
And smooth-chested men
With strong white teeth
Sang gay-sad songs
And drank palm-wine,
The swallows brought
Golden pellets of mud
To build their nests in the rafters.

They knew nothing of what the drummers
Drummed:
Nor the words the singers
Sang.
But they knew something they have always known:
That after the dance
The children will come back to the house
To play with their wooden dolls,
And the grown-ups to their dreams and visions.

Mending Those Nets

They caught the winds in their nets
And brought home a season of plenty.
The unseen hands that mend those nets
Have felt the mornings and the evenings of the sea.

Where the strings have snapped and gone unstrung
Are the years the fish have eaten:
Here are the traps for the winds,
There the doors for the seasons of plenty.

Now is the time to harvest the blue heavens
Wild with the black-striped mackerel
Flashing in the furrows of their foreheads.
Now must they mend those nets,
Now the breezes rattle the coconut palms.

The spirits of their fathers are upon them
And their fingers play a meditation on the strings.

Birth and Rebirth

Clambering over the edge of time
Into the alleys and byways of the night;
Trudging through swampy fevers and wooded dreams;
Marching with the wind in our eyes and hair
Across the cloud-fluffed peaks of hope; through
The blue of the first morning of creation.
Down the dry riverbeds of regret and
The cool and watered paths of temptation,

A woman, a complete stranger, silent,
And determined, led the way and I followed.

In the land where lightning flashed
Persistently searching for thunderbolts
Hurled into hallowed chasms of fire
By centuries of rainstorms, we met some who
Have been where we were bound
And enquired the way of them.

It was always an unseeing stare and a
Pointing of the thumb to the road behind.
Not a word of help nor a smile
Of encouragement; not a flicker of recognition
From those eyes bleached by hunger and thirst
And the things they had failed to see.

Once or twice we took the wrong turning
And retraced our steps,
Noting by markings where we had gone wrong.

At a watering-place we saw birds of prey
Scavenging a massive form—words and axioms
Left to posterity by some unfearing persons.

The vultures rose into the air at our approach
And silence descended between us as understanding.

My guide stood still beside me
As I spied
Through the half-open door of a room
A woman lying on a bed,
With the face of the guide who stood beside me.

Drum Song

Now let my voice imitate the drum
And my hand the drummer's hand.
Let me talk with the accents of the sticks
In the dewy hours of the morning
And in the language of our fathers—

26

You are the milk of the earth.
Do not go sour! Listen.
There is no curse on us. . . .
The fields are clear and rich for new seeds.
Listen.
The fields are clear and rich for new seeds.
The Odum trees are felled but the roots
Cannot be wrenched from the jealousy
Of a loving earth. Listen.

The leaves will sprout again
The leaves will sprout again.

The earth and the sky are wide
The earth and the sky are wide.
Does not the wisdom
Of our elders, the cunning of your artisans,
Frighten the unsuspecting stranger?

You who rise from the bed
Before the palm tree sees the sun,
You—made the path across the stream
So strangers might come like wood-hens
To feed from the cup of your hands
To leave you poorer; to leave you richer.

The earth gives birth to a man and his enemy
But the destruction of the family comes
From the mind of our own clansman,
The tsetse fly must always have blood
In its head; so it hunts and seeks out
Its victims even on the edge of bush-fires.

Asare the beloved is on his sick bed.
Laye cannot drink his medicine for him
Listen—Listen—Listen.

It is only death
Will save us from shame
If our own efforts fail
To fill our hearts, our heads,
And our pots.

A Sandal on the Head[1]

(February 1966)

The broken bones cannot be made whole!
The strong had sheltered in their strength,
The swift had sought life in their speed,
The crippled and the tired heaped out the way
On to the anthills
Had been, bit by bit, half-eaten by termites.
The rough and ready were beginning
To tire of dancing to that one
Strange unfamiliar tune.

The Master of the House cracked his whip
In the realm of laughter and light,
And mopped his brow with a silken cloth.

It is only the gods who know
Why the bones were broken;

It is only the old who know why
The goats skip homeward at evening
And the Master of the House,
Now Master of Rags,
Stays behind on the rocks
To rummage in the rubbish heap
For cast-away morsels of power.

[1] The title of this poem is derived from the Ghanaian custom of touching the chief's head with one of his own sandals to declare him deposed. The poem refers to the downfall of former President Nkrumah.

Dennis Brutus

Though born in Rhodesia, Dennis Brutus went to live in Cape Province, South Africa. He graduated in Arts at Fort Hare University College and subsequently taught English and Afrikaans at Port Elizabeth. As President of the South African Non-Racial Olympic Committee (SANROC), he actively protested against racialism in sport and campaigned for the exclusion of South Africa from the Olympic Games as long as she practised apartheid in sport; and as a result he was banned from teaching and from his university law studies. In 1963 he was arrested but escaped while he was still on bail. Although he had a Rhodesian passport the Portuguese Secret Police in Mozambique handed him over to the South African Security Police. Whilst making a desperate attempt to escape, he was shot in the back in the streets of Johannesburg. When he recovered, he was sentenced to eighteen months hard labour at Robben Island. His poetry has been widely published. In 1962 he was awarded the Mbari prize for poetry and Mbari Publications published his first collection of poems, *Sirens, Knuckles, Boots* (1963) while he was still in prison. His *Letters to Martha* (Heinemann Educational Books, 1968) are poems of his experiences as a prisoner on Robben Island. As he was banned from publishing anything on his release from prison, these poems were written as 'letters' to his sister-in-law, Martha.

Sirens, Knuckles, Boots

The sounds begin again;
the siren in the night
the thunder at the door
the shriek of nerves in pain.

Then the keening crescendo
of faces split by pain
the wordless, endless wail
only the unfree know.

Importunate as rain
the wraiths exhale their woe
over the sirens, knuckles, boots;
my sounds begin again.

Somehow We Survive

Somehow we survive
and tenderness, frustrated, does not wither.

Investigating searchlights rake
our naked unprotected contours;

over our heads the monolithic decalogue
of fascist prohibition glowers
and teeters for a catastrophic fall;

boots club on the peeling door.

But somehow we survive
severance, deprivation, loss.

Patrols uncoil along the asphalt dark
hissing their menace to our lives,

most cruel, all our land is scarred with terror,
rendered unlovely and unlovable;
sundered are we and all our passionate surrender

but somehow tenderness survives.

Our Aims Our Dreams Our Destinations

I

Our aims our dreams our destinations

Thought reconstructed in vacuity

A dialogue:
But God doesn't answer back.

Say then we fear
we hope
we speculate
prognosticate,
what intractable arguments
coil round us
wrestle us Laocoon-like,
and what unnameable horrors
ultimate despair
shudder
and owl-moan hollowly
at the unseen ends
of the dark corridors of the brain.

There looms the threat—
a tight knot forming in the viscera—
of defiant rebellion
so of self-elected damnation—
the only kind a benignant God
makes feasible
—so one feels it
in the tenuous proliferate tendrils of thought.

Well if He damn me,
drive me to damnation
by inflicting the unendurable
force me along the knife-blades till I choose
perdition
how shall I feel guilty?
When my sense of justice says
He drove me
He damned me
He's the guilty one
and if He chose—
BE DAMNED TO HIM

And then to spend eternity
eternally in revolt
against injustice-justice
fighting in vain
against injustice
in the service of my private justice

against a God turned devil
hoping forever for the triumph of despair.
'Evil be thou my Good.'

II

The inherent impulse to good
an inbuilt aspiration
integrated
impossible of disentanglement;
what does it argue?

Is it the seed
from which man grows to divinity
—and, before it,
can God stand condemned?

Before what superior standards
is God found inadequate
His mercy finite and inferior to our own?

And where does compassion
degenerate into sentimentality?

(Pity me! Pity me God! I cry
And imply, not mercy
but a fellow-feeling;
and so?
Impute to him equality
or denigrate his super-humanity
and make it inferior to our own?)

(But he was human once—
or so we are assured
and so can find no human state
beyond the range of his experience
or knowledge:

—but always other depths remain
obscurities of knowledge
divine protectedness,
insulations from our woe)

So we must grapple.

And agony
engenders desperation;
then agnosticism;

then, perhaps
an agonised truth
(truthfulness)

Is He the Infinite Hangman?
Executioner?
Torturer?

Must we be driven to the edge,
racked on the precipice of the world?

For what dread guilt
are these dread exactions made,
the extortion of blood and sighs?

Can we find hope
in thinking that our pain
refines us of our evil dross,
prepares us for a splendid destiny?

or in a fellow-link
a shared enterprise
the splendid Gethsemane
which must purchase redemption for the world
and by our agony
pay debts to buy
the pardon for the world

suffering humanity!
transfigured humanity!
Ecce homo!

Above Us, Only Sky

(Written 5 August 1966, in flight over the Atlantic after leaving
South Africa)

Above us, only sky
below, cloud
and below that
cloud;
below that
sea;
land is abolished,
only the sky and air and light
a beatific approximation
achieved.

After this power
this conquest of brute reality
what can we not do
not abolish?

Peace will come.
We have the power
the hope
the resolution.
Men will go home.

Flight / The Exile / Exit

(For James Cook)

To be thrown outward in a steel projectile
to hurtle outward in quivering uncertainty
to a cold fragment of a continental ledge
for huddling and perching and grubbing
and ultimately, unthinkably, to find settlement there

34

and huddling in this grey tubular box
to find a gathering of the dispersed frantic consciousness
a ragged and stretched fabric of torn anxious mind
no longer struggling to encompass a host of contingencies
but thoughts roosting, still fluttering, on the central
    branched mind

and anger congeals, and becomes aware
partly as the conscious rationale for flight
and partly as the self-conscious indignant pose—
the wounded 'banneling', the D-P type
who is our age's mendicant and jew

anger too that in its artifice holds off
the true deep wound that lies
like the dark bruised pulp at the heart of the fruit:
the agony the heart and mind hold in suspense
the whirling axe—or propeller-blade—whose fierceness
    makes it invisible:

then to alight on green placid earth
to normality and efficient unhostile people
the engines, and all the throbbing straining stilled
and all things quiet, except the dull half-hearted
    throb in the heart. . . .

Paul Chidyausiku

Son of the late Chief Chinamhora, Paul Chidyausiku was born in Rhodesia near Salisbury in 1927. He was educated at Kutama Mission, a secondary school run by Marist Brothers, and at Domboshawa Agricultural School. Taught agriculture for a number of years before joining the Mambo Press in Gwelo in 1960. Has travelled in Europe and in various African countries. Has written five books in his Shona language, published by the Oxford University Press and by Mambo Press. Edits the only paper catering mainly for the African people in Rhodesia.

Grandpa

They say they are healthier than me
Though they can't walk to the end of a mile;
At their age I walked forty at night
To wage a battle at dawn.

They think they are healthier than me:
If their socks get wet they catch a cold;
When my sockless feet got wet, I never sneezed—
But they still think they are healthier than me.

On a soft mattress over a spring bed,
They still have to take a sleeping-pill:
But I, with reeds cutting into my ribs,
My head resting on a piece of wood,
I sleep like a babe and snore.

They blow their noses and pocket the stuff—
That's hygienic so they tell me:
I blow my nose into the fire,
But they say that is barbaric.

If a dear one dies I weep without shame;
If someone jokes I laugh with all my heart.
They stifle a tear as if to cry was something wrong,
But they also stifle a laugh,
As if to laugh was something wrong, too.
No wonder they need psychiatrists!

They think they have more power of will than me.
Our women were scarcely covered in days of yore,
But adultery was a thing unknown:
Today they go wild on seeing a slip on a hanger!

When I have more than one wife
They tell me that hell is my destination,
But when they have one and countless mistresses,
They pride themselves on cheating the world!

No, let them learn to be honest with themselves first
Before they persuade me to change my ways,
Says my grandfather, the proud old man.

I. Choonara

Ismail Choonara comes from Roodepoort, Transvaal, South Africa, and is at present living in England, currently employed as a teacher, doing postgraduate research, writing and painting. He has contributed to a wide variety of periodicals, and his plays have been broadcast by the BBC and German Radio. One of the poets featured in *Seven South African Poets*, edited by Cosmo Pieterse (Heinemann Educational Books).

August 21st, 1968

Yesterday we had a picnic
On the common.

Today is baby's birthday.

The forecast said
It would be fine and sunny.
Did the radio say that
As the tanks rolled in?

Big fish eats little fish
And the world looks on
Like a frightened fisherman.

A Lament for my Step-mother Country

I fear the night
When a white hand flings
A brick.

A window shatters,
A red hand drips
To the sink.

38

Eyes, full of sorrow
Look down.

Fancy patterns on the floor
Of broken glass
Of black blood
Of cheap lino
Of cold shadows
Of words that ring
'Nigger go home,'
    For by your coming
    You have shattered
    My boast.
    I too have prejudices
    That lay dormant
    In distant Bermudan shore.
You came, brought it, exposed it,
And now I am holy no more.
I cannot condemn
I cannot rail
Against petty prejudices that prevail
In other hearts than mine.

    'Nigger go home
    And leave my ideals to me.'

Resurrection

I was searching for Christ
Amongst the Saturday's shopping crowd.
I looked around:
Faces peering,
The vacant stare, the tiredness
Of people who go on, and on,
Mondays to Fridays,
To pay for Saturday's shopping.
I looked to see
If amongst those faces I could find
My Christ:
Faith, hope, charity
And things like that.

I saw a black man, blind.
White stick in black anonymity,
Tap-tapping proboscis,
Hand held by white hand
Across the busy street.
Do I have to look far
For Christ on a Saturday afternoon?

I saw a black child.
Nose dripping, disgustingly, helplessly:
White mucous, globular above the lip.
Sultry, salty taste of childhood memories.
I saw the black head, resting, nesting
Beneath the bosom of a white woman,
Grey-haired, love and tenderness
For a child fostered upon her.
Just the touch of a heavy hand
And a loving heart.
Do I need to look far for Christ:
Saturday's children playing in the park?

Letter to Mamma

Do not ask me
why we are here, mamma.
That is an irrelevancy.
We cannot tell
the difference
between the North
and the South.
Neither could grandpa back home
a hundred years ago
when he was a child.
If it moves
we shoot
straight between
the slanty eyes.
That it is the enemy
of the ideal we are defending.
Do not ask me why.

Fred. You know Fred, mom.
Remember Fred. He is dead.
And Bill was killed on the hill.
Some others you know, mom,
are gone.
But we go on, and on, and on.
We are defending an ideal.
We know it does not sound real,
but here we see clear
the yellow peril in the green jungle
and the red peril in the green jungle,
the flies besides, and the mosquitoes,
the swamps, and the riverboats.
Then there are the bombs, booby traps, bazookas
and a sniper's bullet to stop you dead
in your tracks, mom. Remember Fred.

But we still stick fast, mamma,
because we are defending
the Great Ideal.
But it is so far away from home, mamma,
So far from ideal.

John Pepper Clark

An Ijaw of the Delta area of Nigeria, John Pepper Clark was born in 1935, and educated at Ibadan University where he read English Literature. He founded and edited a poetry magazine, *The Horn*, while a student. He has worked as an editor on a newspaper, conducted research into Ijaw traditional legends under the Institute of African Studies, Ibadan, and is now a lecturer in African Literature at the University of Lagos. John Pepper Clark is one of the most prominent and gifted of the Nigerian poets and playwrights, and recently became co-editor of *Black Orpheus*. In his latest book of poems, *Casualties*, which deals with 'some of the unspeakable events that all but tore apart Nigeria', he tells us that 'I had no previous or prior knowledge of the facts or plans, nor am I altogether convinced that I have all of them correct and complete. But I got so close to a number of the actors after the curtain rose . . . that I came to be identified by some as playing in the show—to the extent of being interrogated by the security people.' Among his publications are *Poems* (Mbari, 1962), *The Song of a Goat* (Mbari), a verse drama performed in 1962, *America, Their America* (Deutsch, 1964), *Three Plays* (O.U.P., 1964), *A Reed in the Tide* (Longman, 1965), *Casualties: Poems 1966-68* (Longman, 1970) and a collection of critical writings on African literature, entitled *The Example of Shakespeare* (Longman, 1972).

The Casualties

(To Chinua Achebe)

The casualties are not only those who are dead;
They are well out of it.
The casualties are not only those who are wounded,
Though they await burial by instalment.
The casualties are not only those who have lost
Persons, or property, hard as it is
To grope for a touch that some
May not know is not there.
The casualties are not only those led away by night;
The cell is a cruel place, sometimes a haven,
Nowhere as absolute as the grave.

The casualties are not only those who started
A fire and now cannot put it out. Thousands
Are burning that had no say in the matter.
The casualties are not only those who escaping
The shattered shell become prisoners in
A fortress of falling walls.

The casualties are many, and a good number well
Outside the scenes of ravage and wreck;
They are the emissaries of rift,
So smug in smoke-rooms they haunt abroad,
They do not see the funeral piles
At home eating up the forests.
They are the wandering minstrels who, beating on
The drums of the human heart, draw the world
Into a dance with rites it does not know.

The drums overwhelm the guns . . .

Caught in the clash of counter claims and charges
When not in the niche others have left,
We fall,
All casualties of the war,
Because we cannot hear each other speak,
Because eyes have ceased to see the face from the crowd,
Because whether we know or
Do not know the extent of wrong on all sides,
We are characters now other than before
The war began, the stay-at-home unsettled
By taxes and rumours, the looters for office
And wares, fearful every day the owners may return,
We are all casualties,
All sagging as are
The cases celebrated for kwashiorkor,
The unforeseen camp-follower of not just our war.

Mbella Sonne Dipoko

Born in Douala, Cameroon, in 1936, Mbella Sonne Dipoko spent part of his childhood on his grandparents' farm at Missaka on the Mingo River. Educated in Cameroon and in Nigeria. He has been a news reporter with the Nigerian Broadcasting Corporation. He is at present living in France, where he worked for a time on the staff of *Présence Africaine*. His poems have appeared in *Présence Africaine*, *Transition* and other journals. His play, *Overseas*, was produced by the BBC and is shortly to be published by Heinemann in *Eleven Short African Plays*.

Our History

And the waves arrived
Swimming in like hump-backed divers
With their finds from far-away seas.

Their lustre gave the illusion of pearls
As shorewards they shoved up mighty canoes
And looked like the carcass of drifting whales.

And our sight misled us
When the sun's glint on the spear's blade
Passed for lightning
And the gun-fire of conquest
The thunderbolt that razed the forest.

So did our days change their garb
From hides of leopard skin
To prints of false lions
That fall in tatters
Like the wings of whipped butterflies.

Romanus N. Egudu

A Nigerian, Dr Romanus N. Egudu took his first degree at the University of Nigeria at Nsukka, and his doctorate at Michigan State University, USA, where the Canadian poet, A. J. M. Smith, supervised his research project. He returned to lecture in the Department of English at Nsukka University. His poems have appeared in *Black Orpheus* and *Transition* and he was represented in both *Commonwealth Poems of Today* (Murray) and *New Voices of the Commonwealth* (Evans).

Look into a Mirror

Look into a mirror,
there you will see
a china vessel, half chalk and half charcoal,
holding flames and ashes,
a lion and a lamb,
a tortoise and a sheep;
an eagle sits looking at a vulture
while a snake eyes a rat,
a hawk crouches next to a chick,
harmattan and rain are playing together,
and night and day sit in council.

Each produces a note in the vessel,
and an organ with the scales
is planted at the core;
place and time play the organ
and weave diverse music:
carols, dirges, symphonies, harmonies,
jazz, high-life, twist . . .

Aigboje Higo

A Nigerian, Aigboje Higo read English at the University of Ibadan, Nigeria, and later did postgraduate work at Leeds University. He taught at St Andrew's College, Oye (in Western Nigeria), for a number of years, and is now Nigerian representative for Heinemann Educational Books. His work has appeared in various literary magazines.

Is It True?

They say because you cut these fingers
you would not trim this nation's conscience.

They say you made one conscience for the rich
another conscience for the poor;

one conscience for religious man
one conscience for free-thinking;

you made a political conscience
and you made a no-conscience.

They say many things, they confound me
God, is it true?

This nation runs a multi-storey conscience.

Fugue for Power

His head is a dunghill
his mind ashes for joy
his feet are a duck's web
his body a baobab trunk.

He slams his webfeet on the fields
he dents rock after rock with his palms
he blows furrows with his nostrils
he lays pools with his ribs.

His meals are a wedding-feast
his yawn is a thunderclap
lions scuttle to safety when he sighs
men desert their safety when he's abroad.

He is a mass of all things
nothing becomes him, nothing delights him
his night and his day are one
he works nothing, his grip is a vice.

Ime Ikiddeh

Born in 1937 at Uyo, South-Eastern State, Nigeria, Ime Ikiddeh graduated in English from the University of Ghana in 1963 and obtained an M.A. in English from Leeds University in 1966. He has since been lecturing in English and African Literature in the University of Ghana. He has published poems in university magazines in Legon and Leeds. Founded the Legon Writers Forum. Edited *Drum Beats* (East African Publishing House), an anthology of African narrative prose.

Martin Luther King

Marcus
Malcolm
Martin
you grandchildren of Uncle Tom
shall we ever know why
white chalk writes so clear
stays so fast on black back-walls?
The dead door of St Peter's
with ninety-nine questions
nailed in your name
knows the pain of questions
awaiting an answer
the men who looted your leave
know you should have lived
where lambs are
whelps of wolves

If you had perched on precipices
walked the steep edge of the sword
you might—who knows?—have lived and lived
then faded to a shade
singing Nunc Dimittis

Every day the world changes in style
like a dance or dress
Every day the world changes
right before our eyes
Here is no place for a walk
Here is no place for a word
the word made flesh
fled from the world
the deed will be louder and louder
where hounds find game refugees
in the silence of the word

Two thousand years is
time enough for a lamb
to change into a charging bull
two thousand years and
cheeks turned for a smack
have bled and
shrivelled into a bone
coal-pot set on the head
has burnt head body and soul
into vapours of smoke and ash
rising in angry clouds and
falling in blood drops
large drops ruddy drops
of fire
will pool and swell into
flaming oceans of hell

Amin Kassam

Born in Mombasa, Kenya, in 1948 and educated at high schools in Mombasa and Nairobi. He spent one year at University College, Nairobi, during which time he was assistant editor of *Busara*, a literary magazine published by the English Department. Took his B.A. Economics (Hons) degree at McGill University, Canada. His poems have appeared in many African magazines and journals, and have been broadcast on the Voice of Kenya programme and by Radio Uganda and the BBC.

Fish

Fish twist through the reeds
Dissolving
Reflections of sky and sun
With their movement
A variety of
Multi-coloured fish
Forming a microcosmic society
Within which my image
Flickers, broken.

June, 1967

Yet once again
Has youthful David hurled
His stone!
'Midst trembling lords
Of Beast and Bird
The Cyclops has struck!

Burning sands
Have whirled and gasped,
And feebly retched
The ooze of curd beneath
The gory vigilance of Death;

The Reaper, hammer sheathed,
Has locked the door
And curtained gazes dunewards,
Hoarse of breath,
At shattered wreckage
On that furnace floor.

The desert cat
Plunged its whiskers in blood,
Licked grisly hairs and gorged,
And now it groans and sickens
Paunch ballooned with crimson mud:

Our sun will rise one day
On brittle bones
And crumbling dust
And green palms.
Then will Man perceive
Man's greatest enemy is Man.

Leper

You now have
your own farm, mother,
wrestled from hyenas
slippery with the blood
of my elder brothers

you have materials enough
to build a house
strong as a baobab,
as inviting as a fire
on a cold night

yet your hands are soft

you let your cousins
farm your land
and corrupt your sons

you let them steal your possessions

you let the thatch rot
in the yard while your sons
bicker over names

while in a corner
I, black sheep,
because of my pigment
stand torn with pain

a leper without a mother

Albert Kayper-Mensah

Born at Sekondi, Ghana, in 1923, Albert Kayper-Mensah was educated at Achimota College and at Cambridge and London Universities. He taught for some years at Wesley College, Kumasi, and is now Cultural Counsellor at the Ghanaian Embassy in Bonn. His poems have appeared in various German literary periodicals and have been broadcast in Germany and Britain.

In God's Tired Face

Each seeking aims
Peculiar to his individual mind
Should keep a record of the find
He makes, however wild the claims;

Some day, by this, maybe
Our world will wake to see
The image of its frightened face
With grim, broken outlines of a tired race,
In the face of God, left on a lady's shawl.

What Will Our Children, Still Unborn . . .

What will our children, still unborn,
hear our critics say of us?
Of our words, fashioned as our sculptors
fashioned wood into masks, dolls, and drums
for healing in thick fetish groves;
of our sculpture that is now collectors' treasure
and the enigma of critics looking
for lost paths where forests grow;
pathways to thought, and sensibilities

53

that guided skilled hands to wild
deformities potent in their influence,
unmasking fears and lighting them
as flaming firebrands that their
bearers rushed into the sea to quench?

Will they say we lacked their merit
or that we were of a piece
in our qualities and stirrings
of the spirit for a voice,
for the things we had to say
and the way we strove to say it?

Will they say we were the heart
of the body of our age,
pumping blood to feed its tissues;
the brain that learns, and guides
bones and muscles, sustaining life;
or a poison, a foreign body
cancerous, destructive, useless?

Will they say we were a sneeze,
a stretch to waken, a yawn, a cough
vital as a safety valve,
or a tear that cleared the eye
once our gathered drops were dry?

Will they say we wrote to live,
and that in us our age lives, too:
or that we had the least to give—
nothing that might encourage you?

Red Earth

(Formal Education)

Red earth
runs red
anywhere,
everywhere.

I am learning:
my subject . . .
no esoteric craft,
no rare, particular object;

any that has turned
out men with minds
made cutlass-sharp
in a skilful farmer's hand;

any that is red earth
for our mother's hearth at home.

Will this book or that
fulfil it?
Will this man or that
inspire it?
Will I swim the way
they teach it?
Will these states of mind
provide it?
Will these ways of thought
ensure it?
Will these exercises
do it?

Red earth
runs crimson
every time, everywhere.

Is it stone that eats the axe
blade to a line of sharpness?
Then it is of red earth.

Train with rope,
swing on wood, throw, and whisk,
swim and climb, fall through air
until your muscles take instructions
with the ease of well-trained dancers,
and your mind,
a far-off moon,
draws your passions high as tides

with a power,
here, near;
until in workshops of experience
you can find a route to peace,
to renewal and release,
contemplation, and to nourishment
of flesh and spirit,
till the hand
outstretched to God
finds a rod
to remove obstacles
and to open doors in walls.

When we have arrived thus far,
we can walk away from home
over any red earth,
knowing as we've always done
that red earth
runs red
every time, everywhere.

Richard Kiya-Hinidza

Born in 1944 in Agbome, a village in the Kpandu District of the Volta Region of Ghana, Richard Kiya-Hinidza was educated at primary and middle schools and a commercial college. He worked in the Civil Service for three years until 1967, and has since been employed as a clerk in the University of Ghana at Legon. His poems have been published in a wide range of Ghanaian papers and periodicals and have been broadcast on Radio Ghana. He is the co-author of a volume of Ewe poems. A member of Legon Writers Forum and of the Ghana Pen and Paper Circle.

African Realism

We are not alone
On this continent of Africa,
Riddled with ideologies unpractised before
And many more yet to be brought
To this land: once a single land—
Now partitioned into colonies
By sons and daughters
Not registered within the family
Of a father whose will we read.
Migrant birds detect before dawn
Where to nest and where not to rest,
On a land not meant for them.
The black soul enjoys the blackness
Of a gloomy forest meant for him:
The secret arts of African witchery,
The sacred arts of his voodoo cults,
Inspirit his enchantment well at home.
But the black chain of African nationalism
Is now patched in gold, copper and bronze,
And the fathers gone now feel restive
When their minds in retrospective digression
See a modern kind of Africa!

Shall we say we are alone
On this continent of Africa
While the migrant birds of the great South
Prefer this borrowed harbourage of ours
To their nature-given home?
Truly, the hermit crab deserts its shell
And borrows yet another shallow shell
To shell its shell-less parts in shame.

We are not alone
On this continent once nicknamed
The Dark Continent (perhaps ever night)
And the 'White-Man's Grave'—perhaps not white-meant.
For the black bats that bark in Congo forests
Do not invite the seagulls to share
In their joy or their unique fate;
Nor will the date-palms of Sahara oases
Sympathise with the oak trees
Who choose the same floor to dance
To the unfamiliar tunes of desert drums.

Yet we are not alone,
Never are we alone on this land—
A modernised kind of upturned Africa,
Where mongrel offspring challenge
The ingenuity of the landowners,
And aliens now on unending holidays
Prefer soon to turn Africaners,
Never to go, never to go back home—
Until that radical time
When a revolution of all Africa
Shall explode in distension;
A time when our hearts shall reach
A point of non-tolerance and belligerency,
A point where the young and the unborn
Will know the cheated and the cheating,
And those forces that intrigue and generate
Inter-state and ethnic tensions exposed
To the judgement of our great forefathers,
The jubilation of our tribesmen,
and the patriotic awareness of our kinsfolk.

We are not alone
In this fight for imitative knowledge.
We have had our national share
Of the wisdom that suits Africa.
While men still relegate us to primitivity,
We ourselves have seen life-samples
Of Eskimos and coloured Indians
Below the grades of semi-civilisation.

We are not alone,
We are not alone in Africa—
Never are we alone in this world
Where the sea and the oceans connect us
With the so-called discovering nations
Living under the same sun, moon and rain.
Let every nation be at its home,
Let every bird in its own nest dwell,
Let the African be free in his home,
And let the searching parties that roam
Stop their search for a lost Africa.

Kojo Gyinaye Kyei

Born in 1932 at Kanyasi No. 2 in the Ahafo Region of Ghana, Kojo G. Kyei was educated at Catholic schools and St Augustine's College, Cape Coast. On the strength of a Cocoa Marketing Board scholarship he went to study Architecture at the University of Kansas, graduating in 1963. He is at present employed as an architect by the Public Works Department of Ghana. He is married and has three children. His poems and articles have appeared in various magazines, and his first collection of poems, *The Lone Voice*, was published by the Ghana Universities Press in 1969.

Alampambo

On one of the crowded sidewalks
   of the Makola Market,
once I came upon a man
   with a million-and-one stitches
   in his i-taya shirt and knickers.
He smiled and smiled all the time.
He had a bowl with rings
   on the rim;
and an old mouth organ
   which he blew into
and danced to his song:

Alampambo
   hwee-hoo hwee-hoo
Alampambo
   hwee-hoo hwee-hoo

This was a beggar,
   but he was a chooser;
for he would dance
   only from three pesewas up
given him in alms:

Alampambo
   hwee-hoo hwee-hoo
Alampambo
   hwee-hoo hwee-hoo

He would stand at one end
   of a sidewalk stretch
cleared of hawkers,
   raise up one arm
to signify all-set-to-go,
   then smile, sing and blow
into his beat-up mouth organ:

Alampambo
   hwee-hoo hwee-hoo
Alampambo
   hwee-hoo hwee-hoo

With tens of people gathered
   watching him
he would stoop and dance
   sideways along the sidewalk stretch,
manfully stamping the ground
   on a jump-dance syncopated beat,
shaking his ring-rimmed bowl
   and singing and blowing
into his old mouth organ:

Alampambo
   hwee-hoo hwee-hoo
Alampambo
   hwee-hoo hwee-hoo

To Sing in My Own Tongue

To sing in my own tongue,
   louder than a faint soft knock
of the debt collector,
   is my wish.

In all these words
    for whoever may pass my way:
    to feel
    to gaze
    to sneer
    to laugh
    to ponder
the pomp of Odikro
    sitting in state;
and the unhurried abandon
    of naked urchins
rioting in the dusty streets of Nwamahinso;
    and village love-hunt
by the hurricane lamp,
    while the moon sleeps.

Just as Eliot inscribed in English
    private words
to his wife in public;
    And Pasternak painted
the Vorobyev Hill in Russian;
    And Apollinaire immortalised
the beauty of his
    lover's hair in French.
        Nanso, ogya ahye
        asanso akyi:
        na m'asemsusu nso
        aka me tirim.
And so if I do,
    you will hear me faintly,
much too faintly.

Blame it on Captain and Crew

Don't look into the eyes
    of ruthless guests
    for *raison d'être* of our plight
    of consuming fire.
Blame it on our vain echelons
    who refuse to change;

blame it on captain and crew
   who don't care two hoots
   where we land.

Don't look for scapegoats
   for the mess
   our own hands wring.
When the damage
   is already done
we can always make
   a fresh start,
sincerely resolved
   selflessly to build
   for far tomorrow.

Don't shift your share
   of corrective axe
   on to the shoulders
   of the other man.
Motherland is a country
   of humans;
and you are *one*.

Let us not fear
   to die a little
for our country
   in the cause we cherish.
We are already dying
   the moment
   we are born.

Common Six Feet of Ground

Nigerian or Burmese,
They all beat their wives.
One difference is that
The Burmese think crickets are
Top of the Pops,
While the Nigerian says snails are
Pop of the tops.

Ghanaian or Philippino,
They all scratch their backs.
One difference is that
The Philippino has rice
For breakfast, for lunch, for dinner;
While the Ghanaian has plantain
For breakfast, for lunch, for dinner.

Briton or Chinese,
They all sneeze in loud or soft
Whiiizzzzimmmm buuummmms!
One difference is that
While the British are fantastic
In *abinkyi* calculations
With knives and forks,
The Chinese can really swing
On the jitterbug of chopsticks.

American or Mexican,
They all can get their steps
Scrambled up at
The sight of a gorgeous girl.
One difference is that
The American like hot dogs real good,
While the Mexican can
Really go to town on tortilla.

Malaysian or Norwegian,
They all eat frog legs.
One difference is that
One is Malaysian
And the other is Norwegian.

Brazilian or Russian,
They all drink beer.
As to the intensity of
The belch each can *eeeaaauuu*,
So far, it has always been
A drawn game.

Cuban or Trinidadian,
They all spank their children.

One difference is that
The Cuban is hard to beat
On the Cha Cha Cha,
While the Trinidadian is
Fully at home on the steel band.

Tanzanian or Congolese,
They all chew bones.
As to the hotness
They charge their dishes with pepper,
Koo,
I say, each is still tough in
The high voltage zone.

Foreigner or native,
What difference is there,
Knowing we all share
This common six feet
Of ground!

The Tough Guy of London

Seen from within a heated room,
On a sunny February afternoon,
London looks like
Any other summer's day.

Step out in only
Your shirt and trousers
And, even, with a black belt in *karate*,
An invisible tough guy
With blimey cold hands and feet,
Punches you
Smack on the nose
Straight back in.

Eric Mazani

Born in the Inyanga district of Rhodesia in 1948. Awarded a full
scholarship at Bernard Mizeki College in Marandellas. Now teaches at
a rural mission school. Poems published in college and literary
magazines and collections in Rhodesia. Edited the college magazine.
Writes in both Shona and English.

Naming the Child

A new sister has been born in my family.
A week passes and people come continually, saying
    'Makorokoto! Congratulations!'
I know they are very happy, but some only want to feast!
We say 'Makombora' in Chimanyika. It is the birth
    festival in English.
This day comes after two weeks. I shall be happy.
I shall eat and eat bread.
The big blue cock will die.
I am sorry but the meat I shall eat, enjoying it.
Tapona is the name of my new sister.
My mother gives her the name meaning 'We have survived'.
She suffered from unknown sickness before Tapona's birth.
My grandmother calls her 'Shupai'.
She is mocking at my father who always came and
    troubled my mother in pregnancy.
My elder sister says she must be called 'Mwarianesu'
    meaning 'God is with us'.
'That is too long, Mhani', I groan, sitting on my low,
    round stool.
At last I declare that she is 'Tapona Shupai'.
I have baptised her with words only.
Next month I shall call her 'Mary' in honour of
    our Lord's Mother.

66

Food is prepared and the names are called by everyone.
My sister is being touched by all present.
Even by that ugly old witch too! She wishes to put
  ill-fortune on the child!
My mother once told me that this woman killed my
  young brother.
What an evil old crone it is now smiling at her!
'May I touch her, too?' I enquired.
She hands the child to me and I go out with her.

The great eaters are there, happy to be eating food.
Rough, greedy, uncaring people.
The birth-feast ends and all go away.
Quiet, silent, decent home it is, very happy with the
  new girl-child.
My father is away and I shall write to him soon.
My father was mocked at, he being absent.
He was mocked at by my kind, ever-joking grandmother.
A new sister has been born to my family.
We are all very happy.

African Dancing

Where are the old men and the old women?
Dead, are they?
Those old savage dancers!
Half-naked, half-mad, and a quarter-drunk!
At the beginning beer was brought but not drunk.
After a long time it was all finished.
They were great drunkards but bound by custom.
Today it has all gone—destroyed!
Our grandparents jive, rock and twist!
What can we do?
Look for skins, drums, feathers and ropes?
My grandmother is a specialist,
A dancer who can leap six feet.
What can amuse us more than this?
This cruel, physical, savage dancing—
There is no more of it today.
We now drink orange juice and forget.

Our muscles, brains and blood cry for our own dancing.
I remember five girls whom I saw—
Their breasts hanging towards the ground,
Their backs well-oiled with milk-fat
Their feet anointed and of sweet colour.
My eyes never changed direction.
That was African dancing!

Where are the drums and the drummers?
Where are the huge clay pots of beer?
Where are the beautifully decorated faces of the women?
Can we let all these things pass?
I shall not. I am in need of them.
I am shy to tell my friends that I love them.
May the spirits on mountains descend.
We are thirsty for dancing and drinking.
We are your sons and your daughters.
Come upon us and heal the dying tradition—
The dying tribal dancing of you, our first fathers!

John Mbiti

John Mbiti was born in Kenya during the colonial days, and educated at Makerere College in Uganda, Barrington, USA, and Cambridge, England, where he obtained his Ph.D. in Theology. He has worked in an Anglican parish in England, and as a visiting lecturer in Birmingham and in Hamburg. His publications on Religion and Literature include *Akamba Stories* (1966), *African Religion and Philosophy* (1969), *Poems of Nature and Faith* (1969), *Concepts of God in Africa* (1970), *New Testament Eschatology in an African Background* (1970), all published by East African Publishing House, and other books and articles. He has been Professor and Head of the Department of Religious Studies at Makerere University College since 1968.

The Funeral

Here let his listless limbs abide
Wrapped in the blanket of eternal silence
Resting beneath a weedy mould

Not these your salty tears
Nor all your solemn mourning songs
Will ever him arouse;
Forever has he fled
To the fulness of the eternal Lord

So raise your mortal eyes
Beyond the horizon of thickening mist
And courage firmly clasp
Till all your journey is writ
From here to mansions far
Where on immortal bed he lies

Walking Backwards

I am tired of walking below my head,
Always bearing the body upon my feet,
Always walking beneath my head.

I am tired of walking behind my nose,
Tired of its leading me, in every path I take.
I'll walk backwards,
And leave my nose to follow last.

I am tired of turning my neck,
Turning it to stare at every lapsing sight.
I'll never never turn it more.
I'll walk stiff and never talk,
To let you see for me,
And talk your love to me.

O Lord, my neck is tired,
Tired of turning to things around:
    Let it stiff become
    And only face
    One long, long way
    The way You will me go.

I am tired of hearing,
hearing cars and trucks and trains,
Veeerryyy tired,
And almost dead
From these noisy tinklings
Deafening me.

Lord, dial me and tune me
To hear but only You.
I am tired from being enticed
By worldliness without
And selfishness within.
O Lord, telephone me
And stillen me,
Stir me up with your colossal love,

Then will I laugh
Everlastingly!

The Snake Song

Neither legs nor arms have I
But I crawl on my belly
And I have
Venom, venom, venom!

Neither horns nor hoofs have I
But I spit with my tongue
And I have
Venom, venom, venom!

Neither bows nor guns have I
But I flash fast my tongue
And I have
Venom, venom, venom!

Neither radar nor missiles have I
But I stare with my eyes
And I have
Venom, venom, venom!

I master every movement
For I jump, run and swim
And I spit
Venom, venom, venom!

Edgar Musarira

Born in Inyanga district of Rhodesia in 1938. Educated at St Augustine's, Penhalonga, and Gwelo Teachers' Training College. Married, with two children. Teaches at Highfield Secondary School, Rhodesia. Poems in Rhodesian magazines and collections.

Cold

The unseen lion
Prowling in the country boy's skin,
Never biting with sharp teeth
Though biting to the marrow.

He walks briskly across fields to school
And with the power of the wind you blast him in the face,
Making ashen white furrows.

Morn after morn
You crack his soles
And cramp his ankles
Layered with dirt of ages.

Parents, woollen the country kids in winter,
Feed them on fat
To stand them brisk against the cold.

Abioseh Nicol

Born in Sierra Leone in 1924, Abioseh Nicol (Davidson S. H. Nicol) was educated in Nigeria and Sierra Leone. He read Natural Sciences at Cambridge. His short stories, articles and poems have been published both in the United States and Europe. Formerly Principal of Fourah Bay College in Sierra Leone, Abioseh Nicol is now a member of the Permanent Mission of Sierra Leone to the United Nations. The following poem was written on a United Nations Mission to Africa.

Words of Wisdom and Love

Words are like oyster shells
Many see only their outer hardness
But the wise hold and open them
And sometimes find within them hidden pearls.

Words are like lightning strokes
Many see only frightening flashes
But the wise pause and wait
And hear the echo of their great thunder

Words are like moonflowers by day
Many see only their bunched leafy fists
But the wise linger till after twilight
And watch them open spilling out their sweet fragrance

Words are like high towering waves
Many see only the hurl of their long angry curl
But the wise stand waiting by the white sand
And feel the gentle soothing trickle of their spent force

So, Africa, when you say to me
In quiet urgency you love me
(Oh you are a torn confused and ravaged land
Your strange uncertain love like shifting tides)
That I must stay and serve your needs
I pause and ponder
I stop and wonder

Perhaps you hold within you
Some hidden gleaming pearl
Some future majesty
Some strange sweet fragrance of moonlit nights
I walk along your foam-flecked shores
Your words hold promise
And are not empty
I have gained wisdom and shall wait

E. Latunde Odeku

Born in Nigeria in 1927, Professor E. Latunde Odeku was educated in the United States of America. He is a neurosurgeon and Professor of Surgery at the University of Ibadan. He is married and has two children. His publications include many scientific and medical books, as well as two volumes of poetry, *Twilight Out of the Night* and *Whispers from the Night*.

Without Diary

(An old Yoruba village)

Men for centuries hid their faces,
They lived their day and passed their way;
And behind them, without page,
Some ashes lay unmarked in deep hard rocks,
Or floated and were washed away.

And so they left no messages
    that they once were here . . .
Men without a past
Secretly, they died away
Each band of tribesmen
    laid their little tools about,
And buried their presence without claim.

Civilisations, dug deep and dark,
Their glorious hidden reigns unknown . . .
Cultures (their diaries unkept):
Who can read, who can hear
The faint and whispered language of the past?

Benedict Oguto

Born in 1944 on the northern shores of Victoria Nyanza, Kenya, Onyango Benedict Oguto was educated at St Theresa's School, Kisumu, and at St Mary's School, Yala. Formerly an assistant store-keeper with a Nairobi motor firm, and then manager of Afrobooks at the Inter-Continental Hotel, he now works at the headquarters of the East African Publishing House in Nairobi. His work has appeared in various literary journals, and his *Keep My Words*, a book of Luo tales, myths, legends and rumours, will appear shortly. His career began when he read some of his verse at the Kisumu Festival of the Arts in 1968.

Queens

A dealer knows the date, my girl;
A dealer knows the date.
Your lips redder than oxpecker's bill,
Your body soft like silk and wool,
Your hair a puppet of fitful wind,
Black cloud flying high aloft.
Black, black . . .
Your head adorned with horse-hair ligisa,
Ligisa of the dead.

Declining gifts of love and life,
I'll celibate die—artful, slippery,
Courting and loving ever,
Mating and wedding never.

City girl, you bleach God's blackness,
You slough your dress of chameleon hue,
You stand there, Queen of heart and purse,
Big wheels swinging at your ears.

76

Your love . . . it rusts so soon.

A dealer knows the date, my girl,
A dealer knows the date.
Car gone
Fridge gone
Flat gone
All rentful
Stripped to bare, you show clean heels.
Celibate, celibate, celibate,
Return where I began:
A dealer knows the date, my girl,
A dealer knows the date.

And lo you are gone! Gone with the waves of life.
Queens are waves of the lake,
Rippling lovely with minor winds
And ending on rocks and lake banks
Splashing with a violent life.

Albert Ojuka

Born in 1945 at Nyanza, Kenya, Albert Ojuka was educated at the Alliance High School, Kikuyu, just outside Nairobi, partly under Carey Francis. He is at present working in Nairobi as a sales representative with Trans-World Airlines. He was a contributor to *Drum Beat* (East African Publishing House) and hopes to have his first collection of poems published shortly. He has also contributed poems and articles to a wide variety of magazines.

Night

In a state of siege
I lie. The thunder explodes
In the wake of downward bursts
Of some skyborne welder's charring light
And warns me of a coming doom.
Then the patter of raindrops
On a left-out basin
Reminds me of the left-out calves.

Quickly I rise
From my creaking papyrus mat
And into the darkness
My fingers probe in aid of blind eyes.
I light the mkebe lamp, and the darkness
Recedes, but quickly closes in again
Like the water whose waves
Rush back to fill the hold of a splash.

As I make to unlatch the bamboo door
The heavy footsteps
Of the village wizard,
Deliberate, slowly passing by my hut,
Also warn me of risks not to take.

The hairs on my head
Smart up and point away
Like those on a cat's mane
When it senses the ominous
Presence of a dog.

Then I hear the loud breaking of a bone,
Then the slow dragging away
Of a body freshly dead, limp,
And I know
Above the gathering weight of the storm
The leopard once again
Has used the charisma of its night-power
To nail me down
In front of my waning lamp.

But, people,
Although the brave crow
Of the father-cock
May be shattered across
The vastness of silent night,
Although the voice of courage
May be wrung to one last yawn
Remember!
The mere shaking of your fists
May set loose
The waters of this static dam
And sweep away the stones
That lie in our way.

John Okai

John Okai was born in Ghana in 1941. He took his M.A.(Litt.) degree from the Gorky Literary Institute, Moscow, in 1967, and was in the Soviet Union for six years. After leaving the Soviet Union he spent a year in Ghana, where he was awarded a postgraduate scholarship at the University of Ghana. He is at present in London, preparing a thesis on Dostoevsky for the School of Slavonic Studies at the University of London. John Okai was invited to give a solo reading of his work at the First Pan-African Cultural Festival in Algiers in 1969. He is a Fellow of the Royal Society of Arts and a Member of the Royal Society of Literature. His poems have been widely published in international literary magazines, and he has read his work to radio and television audiences in West Germany, the Soviet Union, Ghana, Algeria, France and Britain. His first collection of poems, *Flowerfall*, was published by the Writers Forum in London in 1969.

Freedom Symphony

(To Mavis Araba Eduaba)

While yet I breathe!
While yet I breathe—
Through the pores of my skin,
Through the joints in my knees,
Why not leave me to sing:
Of the stillness of the stone
And the gangling of the gourd,
Of the shadow of the star
And the greatness of the grain,
Of the singing of the storm
And the greenness of the grass,
Of the sinking of the seed
And the wobbling of the worm,

Of the shaking of the shade
And the wildness of the wasp,
Of the slowness of the snail
And the weakness of the weed;
Why not leave me to live,
While yet I breathe,
Like the others around?

While yet I breathe!
While yet I breathe—
Through the hairs of my head,
Through the gate of my mouth,
Why not leave me to look:
On the bravery of the broom
And the highness of the hill,
On the blooming of the bud
And the howling of the horn,
On the bareness of the air
And the hovering of the hawk,
On the bleeding of the breeze
And the heaving of the hoe,
On the bending of the bow
And the lingering of the leaves,
On the boldness of the bee
And the laughing of the loom;
Why not leave me to live,
While yet I breathe,
Like the millions I meet?

While yet I breathe!
While yet I breathe—
Through the nails of my toes,
Through the lids on my eyes,
Why not leave me to hear:
Of the fullness of the fields
And the thinness of the thorn,
Of the flapping of the flag
And the tapering of the trunk,
Of the fretting of the frog
And the thickness of the thatch,
Of the fleetness of the fly
And the toughness of the teak,

Of the freshness of the fish
And the plainness of the pond,
Of the fighting of the fowls
And the promise of the path;
Why not leave me to live,
While yet I breathe,
Like the others I know?

While yet I breathe!
While yet I breathe—
Through the bones of my beak,
Through the lids of my ears,
Why not leave me to think:
On the rawness of the rock
And the brashness of the brook,
On the roundness of the root
And the dewiness of the dawn,
On the rudeness of the rod
And the dearness of the ear,
On the rippling of the reed
And the deckling of the duck,
On the raging of the rain
And the coldness of the clay,
On the wrestling of the waves
And the coursing of the clouds;
Why not leave me to live,
While yet I breathe,
Like the millions I meet?

While yet I breathe!
While yet I breathe—
Through the gills in my jaws,
Through the holes in my nose,
Why not leave me to talk:
Of the sharpness of the spear
And the moanings of the mule,
Of the gropings of the smoke
And the marchings of the moon,
Of the softness of the soil
And the muteness of the mount,
Of the shyness of the sky
And the meekness of the mat,

Of the sourness of the salt
And the wailing of the wind,
Of the skating of the kite
And the cunning of the cat;
Why not leave me to live,
While yet I breathe,
Like the others around?

Dodowa Sonata

Pardon me—
And pardon me please again,
If for the
Past unending hour, with the
Yawning gate
And hostile dog for company
You have stood
There with none to answer
Your knock on
Door, offer you a stool to
Sit on, and
Calabash of cool water from
The village well;
When you enter a house where
The people
Are quarrelling among them
Selves, they
Have not the time and
Patience to
Look to see who it is
That has entered, much less
To look to
See the deer you chased and
Caught alive,
Or to ask to know what
Language you
Share with the stars of the
Night sky, but
If you listen hard enough, you
Will hear the
Smoke deserting this hearth

And this earth,
Fleeing through the thatched roof
Of grandmother's hut,
. . . Singing:
They are selling silence
   And teasing toads,
They are burning boats
   And chewing stones,
They are burning boats
   And fingering lions,
They are buying names
   And laundering lakes,
They are sunning suns
   And slaughtering songs.

And Okomfo Okomfo . . .
You simply do not know
What fishes are flying,
What monkeys are jumping
And what snakes are standing,
Within the Dodowa woods . . .

Kokotako Kokotako . . .
Go and ask your mother—
Kokotako Kokotako . . .
Go and ask brother Hindu.

If you listen hard enough you
Will hear the
Smoke deserting this hearth
And this earth,
Fleeing through the thatched roof
Of my grandmother's hut
. . . Singing:
They are boiling bones
   And killing cobras,
They are chasing clouds
   And retailing tears,
They are pruning skies
   And rejecting hearts,
They are milking mice
   And stoning stars.

And Okomfo Okomfo
You simply do not know
What rains are falling
What donkeys are dancing
And what wires are touching
Within the Dodowa woods . . .

Kokotako Kokotako
Go and ask your mother
Kokotako Kokotako
Go and ask brother Hindu.

Forest Desert

The ribs of
Darkness, like the little fainting
Facts of flesh
Left over on the bones of a
Vulture-visited
Elephant carcase, lie weeping, bleeding
In the lap
Of a moon-contoured world, sitting
Silent over
Lake and stone and stump.   The ribs
of darkness.

You hold your nose
Upon the spine of smoke soaked
In the incense
Of some nonsense salted enough
To the point of
Being innocent of the sour sense
In a sage's
Silent staccato verandah cough.

And you tell me
To turn my toes to where my ears
Hear the hesitant
Heavings of a ritual dance beginning

In the bowels
Of a forest famous for the free
Flow of a blue-boned blood.

I sit here
With my life in my lap, drinking
In by degrees
The drone of a desert deserted
In midstream
By the rainfall of faith in dreams
That almost
Could have been.   Looking on
From where no
Mirage can be seen, the sorry
Skeleton of
A song relayed from a sun that has
Stopped shining
Thunders down unto the desert sands
Like the bony

Remnants of the parachutist who
In midstream
All too late lost his stability in
The death of his centre of gravity.

Rosimaya

You stone
    my Saturdays,
You waste
    my Wednesdays,
And tear up
    my Tuesdays,
Into two:
You snare
    my Sundays,
You squeeze
    my Saturdays,
And toss
    my Tuesdays
On to thorns.

You feign
            you feign
                        you
Feign
    you forget my face
In even
The pious
Presence
Of God our God
The Father Almighty,
The maker
Of heaven and earth,
Including all—
Even you and me
Who today
Both hold on to worlds
As different
As the land from the
Sea!
Why can't you tell
Me
You no more love
Me?
Or why not tell
Me
You can love me no
More?

You scorn
    my Sundays,
You freeze
    my Fridays,
And sink
    my Saturdays
In a swamp;
You wet
    my Wednesdays,
You soil
    my Saturdays,
And milk
    my Mondays
Of their mirth.

You feign
        you feign
            you
Feign
    I did not tell you
The time and
Place we were to meet;
But I know
I know I did tell you.
You did
Repeat it yourself
My witnesses
Are your innocent
Ears, not your
Faithful tongue and eyes
Who'd also
Refuse to remember:
Why can't you tell
Me
You never have loved
Me?
Or why not tell
Me
You just will not love
Me?

You lash
    my Saturdays,
You tease
    my Tuesdays,
And snob
    my Sundays
In the sun;
You mock
    my Mondays,
You wreck
    my Wednesdays,
And smother
    my Sundays
In the smoke.

You feign
      you feign
            you
Feign
  you do so love me
But the truth
Is now like the rain;
He who sees not,
Feels it on his skin,
And with
A deep paralysing pain,
Erodes away
The still-wet walls of
Our strong castles
Built in my dreams.
The terrible truth
Is not like the sun—
Where it is
Not seen, it is felt;
Skin of your words
Show a telltale tan,
Scales blinding
My eyes start to melt.

You foul
  my Fridays,
You starve
  my Saturdays
And mess up
  my Mondays
In the mud;
You shun
  my Saturdays,
You maim
  my Mondays
And heap heavy sorrow
Onto my soul.

Gabriel Okara

Born in 1921 in the Ijaw district of the Delta region of Nigeria, Gabriel Imomotime Obainbaing Okara was educated at Government College, Umuahia, Nigeria. After leaving school he continued to educate himself. He served as Information Officer with the Eastern Regional Government in Enugu for a period. His poems and short stories have been broadcast, and published in many literary magazines and anthologies. His novel, *The Voice*, was published in 1964 by André Deutsch and he was one of the four poets featured in *Poetry from Africa*, edited by Howard Sergeant (Pergamon Press, 1968).

Once Upon a Time

Once upon a time, son,
they used to laugh with their hearts
and laugh with their eyes;
but now they only laugh with their teeth,
while their ice-block-cold eyes
search behind my shadow.

There was a time indeed
they used to shake hands with their hearts;
but that's gone, son.
Now they shake hands without hearts
while their left hands search
my empty pockets.

'Feel at home,' 'Come again,'
they say, and when I come
again and feel
at home, once, twice,
there will be no thrice—
for then I find doors shut on me.

So I have learned many things, son.
I have learned to wear many faces
like dresses—homeface,

officeface, streetface, hostface, cock-
tailface, with all their conforming smiles
like a fixed portrait smile.

And I have learned, too,
to laugh with only my teeth
and shake hands without my heart.
I have also learned to say, 'Goodbye',
when I mean 'Good-riddance';
to say 'Glad to meet you',
without being glad; and to say 'It's been
nice talking to you', after being bored.

But believe me, son.
I want to be what I used to be
when I was like you. I want
to unlearn all these muting things.
Most of all, I want to relearn
how to laugh, for my laugh in the mirror
shows only my teeth like a snake's bare fangs!

So show me, son,
how to laugh; show me how
I used to laugh and smile
once upon a time when I was like you.

You Laughed and Laughed and Laughed

In your ears my song
is motor car misfiring
stopping with a choking cough;
and you laughed and laughed and laughed.

In your eyes my ante-
natal walk was inhuman, passing
your 'omnivorous understanding'
and you laughed and laughed and laughed.

You laughed at my song,
you laughed at my walk.

Then I danced my magic dance
to the rhythm of talking—
drums pleading, but you shut your
eyes and laughed and laughed and laughed.

And then I opened my mystic
inside wide like
the sky, instead you entered your
car and laughed and laughed and laughed.

You laughed at my dance,
you laughed at my inside.

You laughed and laughed and laughed.
But your laughter was ice-block
laughter and it froze your inside, froze
your voice, froze your ears,
froze your eyes and froze your tongue.

And now it's my turn to laugh;
but my laughter is not
ice-block laughter. For I
know not cars, know not ice-blocks.

My laughter is the fire
of the eye of the sky, the fire
of the earth, the fire of the air,
the fire of the seas and the
rivers fishes animals trees,
and it thawed your inside,
thawed your voice, thawed your
ears, thawed your eyes and
thawed your tongue.

So a meek wonder held
your shadow and you whispered:
'Why so?'
And I answered:
'Because my fathers and I
are owned by the living
warmth of the earth
through our naked feet.'

Christopher Okigbo

Born in Ojoto, near Onitsha in Eastern Nigeria, in 1932, Christopher Okigbo was educated at Government College, Umuahia, and Ibadan University, where he took a degree in Classical Languages. From 1956 to 1958 he was Private Secretary to the Federal Minister of Research and Information and then taught for a couple of years before taking an appointment as Librarian at the University of Nigeria at Nsukka. Later became Nigerian representative for Cambridge University Press. In his poetry we can see the merging of cultures, of old and new, of personal and universal, of the African and Western worlds. He was killed in battle at Akwebe in September, 1967, on the Nsukka sector of the war in Nigeria. He was a member of the editorial board of *Black Orpheus* and one of the most intellectual of the African poets. His death was a tragedy, not only for Nigeria, but for us all. His publications include: *Heavensgate* (Mbari, 1962), *Distances* (Mbari, 1964), *Limits* (Mbari, 1964), *Silences* (Mbari, 1965) and *Path of Thunder* (Mbari, 1968). He contributed to both *Commonwealth Poems of Today* (Murray) and *New Voices of the Commonwealth* (Evans). A posthumous collection of his complete poetic works, *Labyrinths with Path of Thunder*, was published by Heinemann in association with Mbari in 1971. The poem which follows is one of the last poems he wrote.

Elegy of the Wind

White light, receive me your sojourner; O milky way,
   let me clasp you to my waist;
And may my muted tones of twilight
Break your iron gate, the burden of several centuries,
   into twin tremulous cotyledons . . .

Man of iron thrust—for I will make broadcast with
   eunuch-horn of seven valves—
I will follow the wind to the clearing,
And with muffled steps seemingly out of breath break
   the silence the myth of her gate.

For I have lived the sapling sprung from the bed
   of the old vegetation;
Have shouldered my way through a mass of ancient
   nights to chlorophyll;

Or leaned upon a withered branch,
A blind beggar leaning on a porch.

I have lived the oracle dry on the cradle of a new
      generation . . .
The autocycle leans on a porch, the branch dissolves into
      embers,

The ashes resolve their moments
Of twin-drops of dew on a leaf:
And like motion into stillness is my divine rejoicing—
The man embodies the child
The child embodies the man; the man remembers
The song of the innocent,
Of the uncircumcised at the sight of the flaming razor—

The chief priest of the sanctuary has uttered
   the enchanted words;
The bleeding phallus,
Dripping fresh from the carnage cries out for
   the medicinal leaf . . .

O wind, swell my sails; and may my banner run
   the course of wider waters:

The child in me trembles before the high shelf on the wall,
The man in me shrinks before the narrow neck of a calabash;

And the chant, already all wings, follows
In its ivory circuit behind the thunder clouds,
The slick route of the feathered serpent.

Okot p'Bitek

Born in 1931 at Gulu in Northern Uganda, Dr Okot p'Bitek was educated at Gulu High School and King's College, Budo. He read Education at the University of Bristol, Law at the University of Aberystwyth and Social Anthropology at Oxford. He subsequently lectured at Makerere University College, Uganda. He has played football for Uganda. Founder of the Gulu Festival. His Lwo novel, *Lak Tar*, was published in 1953. His poems and articles have appeared in a variety of East African magazines. *Song of Lawino* (from which the extracts below were taken) is a satire on modern Africa. He is at present Director of the National Cultural Centre of Uganda.

My Name Blew Like a Horn Among the Payira

(From *Song of Lawino*)

I was made chief of girls
Because I was lively,
I was bright,
I was not clumsy or untidy,
I was not dull,
I was not heavy and slow.

I did not grow up a fool
I am not cold
I am not shy
My skin is smooth
It still shines smoothly in the moonlight.

When Ocol was wooing me
My breasts were erect.
And they shook
As I walked briskly,
And as I walked
I threw my long neck
This way and that way
Like the flower of the *lyonno* lily
Waving in a gentle breeze.

And my brothers called me *Nya-Dyang*
For my breasts shook
And beckoned the cattle,
And they sang silently:

    Father prepare the kraal,
    Father prepare the kraal,
    The cattle are coming.

I was the Leader of the girls
And my name blew
Like a horn
Among the Payira.
And I played on my bow harp
And praised my love.

Ocol, my husband,
My friend,
What are you talking?
You saw me when I was young.
In my mother's house
This man crawled on the floor!

The son of the Bull wept
For me with tears,
Like a hungry child
Whose mother has stayed long
In the simsim field!

Every night he came
To my father's homestead,
He never missed one night

Even after he had been beaten
By my brothers.

You loved my giraffe-tail bangles,
My father brought them for me
From the Hills in the East.

The roof of my mother's house
Was beautifully laced
With elephant grass;
My father built it
With the skill of the Acoli.

You admired my sister's
Colourful ten-stringed loin beads;
My mother threaded them
And arranged them with care.

You trembled
When you saw the tattoos
On my breasts
And the tattoos below my belly button;
And you were very fond
Of the gap in my teeth!

My man, what are you talking?
My clansmen, I ask you:
What has become of my husband?
Is he suffering from boils?
Is it ripe now?
Should they open it
So that the pus may flow out?

I was chief of youths
Because of my good manners,
Because my waist was soft.
I sang sweetly
When I was grinding millet
Or on the way to the well
Nobody's voice was sweeter than mine!
And in the arena
I sang the solos

Loud and clear
Like the *ogilo* bird
At sunset.

Now, Ocol says
I am a mere dog
A puppy,
A little puppy
Suffering from skin diseases.

Ocol says
He does not love me any more
Because I cannot play the guitar
And I do not like their stupid dance,
Because I despise the songs
They play at the ballroom dance
And I do not follow the steps of foreign songs
On the gramophone records.
And I cannot tune the radio
Because I do not hear
Swahili or Luganda.

What is all this?

My husband refuses
To listen to me,
He refuses to give me a chance.
My husband has blocked up my path completely.
He has put up a road block
But has not told me why.
He just shouts
Like house-flies
Settling on top of excrement
When disturbed!

My husband says
He no longer wants a woman
With a gap in her teeth,
He is in love
With a woman
Whose teeth fill her mouth completely
Like the teeth of war-captives and slaves.

The Graceful Giraffe Cannot Become a Monkey

My husband tells me
I have no ideas
Of modern beauty.
He says
I have stuck
To old-fashioned hair styles.

He says
I am stupid and very backward,
That my hair style
Makes him sick
Because I am dirty.

It is true
I cannot do my hair
As white women do.

Listen,
My father comes from Payira,
My mother is a woman of Koc!
I am a true Acoli
I am not a half-caste
I am not a slave-girl;
My father was not brought home
By the spear
My mother was not exchanged
For a basket of millet.

Ask me what beauty is
To the Acoli
And I will tell you;
I will show it to you
If you give me a chance!

You once saw me,
You saw my hair style
And you admired it,
And the boys loved it.
At the arena

Boys surrounded me
And fought for me.

My mother taught me
Acoli hair fashions;
Which fits the kind
Of hair of the Acoli,
And the occasion.

Listen,
Ostrich plumes differ
From chicken feathers,
A monkey's tail
Is different from that of the giraffe,
The crocodile's skin
Is not like the guinea fowl's,
And the hippo is naked, and hairless.

The hair of the Acoli
Is different from that of the Arabs;
The Indians' hair
Resembles the tail of the horse;
It is like sisal strings
And needs to be cut
With scissors.
It is black,
And is different from that of white women.

A white woman's hair
Is soft like silk;
It is light
And brownish like
That of the brown monkey,
And is very different from mine.
A black woman's hair
Is thick and curly;
It is true
Ring-worm sometimes eats up
A little girl's hair
And this is terrible;
But when hot porridge
Is put on the head

And the dance is held
Under the sausage-fruit tree
And the youths have sung

You, Ring-worm,
Who is eating Duka's hair
Here is your porridge,

Then the girl's hair
Begins to grow again
And the girl is pleased.

Lenrie Peters

Born in Bathurst, The Gambia, in 1932, and educated there, in Freetown and at Trinity College, Cambridge, Lenrie Peters qualified as a doctor in 1959, and later as F.R.C.S., specialising in surgery in English hospitals for ten years before returning to practise medicine in Africa in 1969. His interest in Pan-Africanism continues, and the pursuit of music and singing. His publications include *Poems* (Mbari, 1964), *The Second Round* (novel, Heinemann Educational Books, 1965) and *Satellites* (poems, Heinemann Educational Books, 1967). A third volume of poems is on the way, and plans are being made for the filming of *The Second Round*.

The River Flowing Soft

The river flowing soft
laguno limbed, folding and unfurling
currents indelible like your hair;
with wrecks and rapids
like the meteor of life
flowing endlessly, softly
into the long distance
where conflicts resolve
and new catastrophes face us.

Empty me of dreams
as she my heart
with fragrant eyes bright perishing
like watching beacons
birds' nests along the river bank
double flanked with zest.

Watching to see the ecstasy
or decline and wondering which.

I have visited Mammon
heard gold coins
murmuring in my jugulars
then turned my face.
How many dig in knives
to find, but silence life for ever?
I have lived in
the hot-house of the flesh
at noon day, and night
has not been strange.

Where in this calendar
of errors do I recline
to shed a tear
or raise my hand in prayer?
Too gross for sane computers
madness and infirmity
madness and infirmity
threaten all who hope for better things.

River flowing gently curling
my blood in sure advance
I will rest now
as do your mysteries
at evening. But when
the sun flash rides the sky
I will again with questions why?

The First Incision

The first incision
leaves the body never quite the same
the broken window-pane
gales, frost, the sweet insouciance of pain

At the inception
we traverse Bluebeard's mansion

open to all except the last door
the final flaw

Though battle-scarred
shut out, the bending strain
of rags upon my back
I would not alter track

I go, return to the
infinitude of my consciousness
its disarray of monuments
where no trespassers come

I would not speak the word
heavy on every lip spewed out
though sunsets blaze in my heart
the voice chokes with longing

Love, you have conquered the world
held mankind in chains
slippery disguise of a word
impaled upon a cross

The old man in a dungeon
what does he understand
of roving legs bedrenched
on Hampstead Heath

Okigbo for love of tribe?
Where now your jewelled talent
roaring at the door Soyinka
for love of principle?

I have seen much of tears
dangling willows at the water's edge
but no abiding pledge
the black rose will be fed

No tortures of flesh can touch you now
approximate to the fires of the heart
which has roamed the confines of death
seen outlines of immortality

What Magic Spells

What magic spells
held the first man,
wandering in darkness,
heads bowed, to draw
breath, refuge from toil,
and say
This is our home
 Katchikali

And the crocodiles
of another world
under your waters
tame as pumpkins
 Katchikali

Katchikali, Katchikali
the women weight-drowned
towards the farms bend
their knees and say a prayer
 Katchikali

Lovers under a fertile moon
pray for their children
 Katchikali

and the crocodiles, watchful
older than fossils
which kiss the heels of children
 Katchikali

and men strong as baobabs
press-ganged to clear your
dense embraces,
the sweat of fear on their faces,
plead with every fateful stroke—
'It is not I who destroy you
it is not I, *Katchikali*,
but those who would ignore your mysteries.'

Katchikali, Katchikali

bring me children
that I may show my face
in the village market,
I the daughter of despair.

Old men sing songs
when the moon is high
pray for their crops
and homes like waves.

But the new people do not understand
will not understand, *Katchikali*,
and all the institutions crumble.

As the mud hut crumbles
withers, all is base
seething self-interest and corruption
and the demon of gain
in your waters, *Katchikali*.
Hide-hunters will not
leave the peace unbroken
  Katchikali

Katchikali, Katchikali
though the birds make their music
in the morning
we do not hear
though they spill sceptres
in the evening
we do not see
we wither and crumble
weeds in a torrent
  Katchikali

But your wisdom is silent
we call to you
there are no answers
we reach out to you
beyond ineffable darkness.

Children of despair
call out to you, *Katchikali*,

tearing out their virtue
they reach out to you, *Katchikali*,
dying in a forgotten ambience
where ships no longer call
or plough and hoot in haste
but belch warm welcomes
in the night
against the quivering gates
of the new cities of the plain.

You Talk to Me of 'Self'

You talk to me of 'self'
—the African Self. The inner
workings of a man, his caste
the meaning of his life.

Senghor extols the beauty,
the African beauty. The
chocolate icing and mascara 'selves'
along the ports and river's edge.

Go arrow-flight two hundred miles
and ask for 'self', but
when you find him, send
one word so I may see.

Go into villages, not palaces,
look among sheep and goats,
under pyramids of squalor,
degradation, the moon's eclipse.

Octogenarian breasts at twenty
enthroned in pools of urine
after childbirth, whose future
is not theirs to mould or flirt with mirth.

There is your 'Self' crushed
between the grinding wheel
of ignorance and the centuries,
the blood congealed in the baking sun.

Then search your conscience
romantic notions anathematised
Black can be beautiful
without the nibbling away of mice.

Though not through abject laziness
or that erratic genius chance,
but diverted energies from nuptial beds,
hard work and common sense.

Henry Pote

Born at Banga Village, near Ndanga Hospital, in Rhodesia in 1939. Brought up by his grandmother who was a *n'anga* (witchdoctor). Educated at Gokomere Mission. Now reading for his B.A. with the University of South Africa. Since 1961 has taught at various schools in and around Salisbury. Writes in both Shona and English. Poems in Rhodesian magazines and collections.

To My Elders

Old enough am I through the span of years,
Yet neither tribal elder nor settler my opinion hears.
My stand to the one is strange and preposterous
And to the other rampant, immature, boisterous.
Often have I envied my forefathers' ignorance
When cattle, wives and grain meant abundance,
With books, machines and ideologies of no consequence.
Man's destiny lay in Midzimu's indulgence.
My knowledge is impotent power and gone sour.
The old and the new in me shall yet find,
I hope, blended in equal and fine
Measure, both inheritances; if not, bemoan your distrust.
Condemn yourselves in me and die, as you entrust
To me what you denied me when you lived!

The Sun Goes Up and Up

The sun goes up and up—while you beat at drums
And burn up your strength
With undignified and unprofitable dances
—While at home there is not even a stool to sit on.

The sun goes down and down—while you debauch;
Destroying your bowels, intelligence, even your humanity

—While at home your children are starving
—While your hearts delight in thinking your actions are
   pleasing.

Throughout the day and night, the month and year, you kill
   each other,
—While your rivals prepare, putting themselves in readiness;
Young men and women are bleeding and being destroyed
—While old men and women, who have devoured granaries,
   remain.

The sun goes up and up—while you complain
And the clever ones exploit your substance and strength,
Waxing rich—while you are reluctant
To work for yourselves, to help yourselves, to live in harmony.

Praying for New Life

Look! Watch those trees
Delighting in their new leaves and flowers;
They seem to have come to life the day before yesterday . . .
But the rain stopped at the time of harvesting.
From whence then came this shooting of new life?

Look! Observe the snake, the beetles and the cicada awakened
From the sleep of a long night. Creatures leap about
With a new strength. The grass is greening
From its old roots. Look carefully
At the death and resurrection around you and learn about life.

I, too, die and arise daily by sleeping at night
And waking in the morning, yet I am still asleep
Foolishly, since I cannot regain,
Like the leaves, the flowers, and the grass,
The new life which flows from the soil's command.

You, ancestral spirits of our forefathers,
See: the world has changed. Teach me your truth.
I yearn for roots that cannot wither, roots of life
New, in a new world. My old roots have been pulled.
Lord God, give me good water and soil, that I can grow.

Fred Rex Quartey

Born in Accra, Ghana, in 1944, Fred Rex Quartey was educated at the Accra Academy (1959-63) and the University College of Cape Coast (1966-8), where he read Mathematics, Physics and Education. While at university he was a founding member of the Writers' Club and some of his poems were published in the *Tear-Gas* magazine. Some of his poems have appeared in the local weekly *Radio and TV Times* and others have been broadcast over Radio Ghana External Service.

Meditation

When the sellers return from the markets
After they have sold their various wares
And brought home corn to prepare for supper,
We shall sit in groups outside the huts
And tell stories of past glories to the children;
We shall also play games
Until the stars disappear from the sky
And the old women go to sleep in their huts.

It cannot be the hymn we composed
Which is being chanted around the gates:
It is the renewal of neglected friendship
And the reappraisal of our cultural heritage.

Hope

I wait in vain for the day to come,
The day when we shall be assembled
Before the council of the elders
And hear the prophecy of coming events.
We shall daily visit the farm
And plant the remaining grains;

I

We shall also pray for rain
To fall on our barren land.
That night we shall gather at the shores
And watch the fishermen paddle
Their canoes far to sea;
We shall impatiently wait for their safe return,
When we shall celebrate for three long nights
And dance before the sacred shrines,
When children will be chanting war songs
And mothers will be grinding pepper for the
Evening meals
Before the sun gives way to the moon
To lighten our dark doors.

With Trembling Hands

With trembling hands
And troubled minds
We peep into the pot
To read the prophecy
Of the coming days,
And the fruits
Of our labouring days.

We have fought brutally
The great unending wars;
We have slain
All the unknown villagers;
We have missed
The ceremony of
The unborn ones
And the parting away
Of the elderly ones;
We promise absolute support
To your wise utterance.

With trembling hands
And troubled minds
We peep into the pot
To read the prophecy.

Richard Rive

Born in Cape Town in 1931, his father an American negro seaman, his mother a 'Cape Coloured'. Graduated in 1949 as B.A. from the University of Cape Town. At present Richard Rive teaches English Literature and Latin in a high school in South Africa. His short stories have been translated into several languages and have been published in a number of countries, and some of them were published in a volume entitled *African Songs* (Seven Seas, Berlin, 1963). He compiled a collection of short stories by four South African writers under the title *Quartet* (Crown Publishers, New York, 1963), and an anthology brought out by Heinemann. His first novel, *Emergency*, was published in 1964 by Faber.

Where the Rainbow Ends

Where the rainbow ends
There's going to be a place, brother,
Where the world can sing all sorts of songs,
And we're going to sing together, brother,
You and I, though you're white and I'm not.
It's going to be a sad song, brother,
Because we don't know the tune,
And it's a difficult tune to learn.
But we can learn, brother, you and I.
There's no such tune as a black tune.
There's no such tune as a white tune.
There's only music, brother,
And it's music we're going to sing
Where the rainbow ends.

David Rubadiri

David Rubadiri was born in Malawi (then Nyasaland) in 1930. Educated at Makerere College, Uganda, and King's College, Cambridge, where he took the English Tripos. He was detained by the Government during the state of emergency in Nyasaland in 1959. Has been Principal of Soche Hill College, Limbe, and Malawian Ambassador to the USA, and is now teaching at Makerere. His first novel was published in 1967 by the East African Publishing House.

The Tide that from the West Washes Africa to the Bone

The tide that from the west
Washes Africa to the bone
Gurgles through my ribs
And gathers the bones
That clatter into clusters,
Rough and polished,
To fling them back destitute
To the desolate river bank.

The tide that from the west
Tears through the heart sinews of Africa
Boils in my marrow,
Dissolving bone and sinew.

The tide that from the west
Washes the soul of Africa
And tears the mooring of its spirit,
Till blood-red the tide becomes
And heartsick the womb—
The tide that from the west
With blood washes Africa
Once washed a wooden cross.

Christmas 1967

In the void
the full emptiness
that '67 has been;
receiving and returning
snow-piled cards
presents and wishes
and ate turkey.
We also read the news
of 121 mercenaries
fed on turkey
and the Red Cross
Christmas Pie.

The dark skeleton
on the Oxfam card
pleading for something
in South Africa
Vietnam
and Rhodesia.

Christmas '67
Teddy bears
Father Christmas
down African chimneys
on National Television,
hidden presents
in friends' houses
and a coup d'état
to make it dramatic.

At oo something hours
a queen's message
'one mile run by a native—
goodwill to the Commonwealth':
all in the oral tradition.
Then a message
from a friend in Paris
talking about Vietnam
and Major Schramme—

The best Christmas card
as POWER and power
talked over a cocktail jet stop
at the Vatican.

Then we sang orgasmally
Away in a Manger—
Goodwill and Peace to us all
Good Christian people.

Dry hot sands
—hot gun barrels
—dry hard hearts
—finger and trigger
—night clubs
at Mulago maternity
a bumper crop
for Christmas '68.
But the desert still stretching—
scorching;
the camel's hump
still sagging with water.

Poem in Remembrance

I **Christopher Okigbo**

Heavensgate
and *Limits*
who can reach them?
Lead and barrels of heat
do so easily.
Youth and Love
Joy and Faith
have gone through them,
and now our limits
because the lights at heavensgate
have departed.

II **Yatuta Chisiza**

'Old soldiers never die',
the saying goes—
so too to Yatuta,
so too to the cause
he lived for.

For us
the rank and file
only the agony
and the pity
for a piece of lead.

There is much to remember
and little to forget
when greatness
dies a simple death
for souls of men.

John Ruganda

Born in Uganda in 1941, John Ruganda read Literature at Makerere University College. He is at present editorial and sales representative for Oxford University Press in Uganda. He contributed to *New Voices of the Commonwealth* (Evans).

Barricades of Paper Houses

At dusk, mother,
Village crickets chirp
The bruised fortunes
Of the wrinkled;
At dawn
The dew will glitter
Yet another hope
For those born
By mothers of tatters.

At dusk, wrinkled one,
Slum noses twitch
At tiny anthills
Of faeces
Of the children of kwashiakor
And our scorched throats itch
When dogs with deflated stomachs
Hurry to lick shrivelled buttocks
Of the children of kwashiakor.

Yet the tax-men
Will come as usual,
Will come with their chains
And handcuffs
And police-officers;
Our doglets will bark at them,

Will bark at their clean clothes
And their indifference
And we'll go on dodging,
Dodging the handcuffs
And the police-officers
And pailfuls of human dung
In cold prison cells;
We'll go on dodging
And leaping
From dustbins to paper houses
Dilapidated.

What cause have they,
These guardians of indifferent laws,
What cause have they
To leave us alone
With our paper houses
And doglets and babylets?

I now hear the rude clang
Of the town clock tower;
I hear it scattering the twilight
Behind barricades of paper huts.
The rude clang
Scorns my uncertainty
And strips my desolation.
While the shroud of darkness
Lasts
They've no eyes to see,
No eyes to see
Decrepit humans
Who're afraid
To look at themselves
In the light and the mirror.

But now the new day
Will bring those who've auctioned
Their tongues
To buy kinship
Of the disciples of money,
Will bring those who've mortgaged
Their honesty

To buy a right
To lurk in the shadows
Of prisoners of power.

They'll soon file past me
To thumb through files
And morning papers
That carry messages
Of blood and hatred,
New fashions of deaths
And dresses;
They'll file past me
Putting on party faces
And party shirts,
Counting their shuffles indifferently;
And I'll go on huddled here
Behind barricades of dustbins
Till the guardians of handcuffs
And pailfuls of human dung
Consume themselves in liquor.
I'll go on feeding
On the communal stench
Around this place,
The place that's unmindful
Of beatings of a soul
Beaten.

Michael Sequeira

Born in Uganda, in 1950, of Indian parents, Michael Sequeira was educated at local schools and in 1970 sat for the 'A' level examinations of the Cambridge University Examinations Council, with Literature, Economics and Geography as his main subjects. This is the first poem he has had published.

They Bathe in the River

Down by the river,
the mobile picture of transition,
from snow chunks at the mountain-top
and the glacial precipitation on the slopes
to the crystal-clear water
that flows downstream undaunted,
sit
bare-bodied villagers
already wet,
showing faint lustre
like oiled sculpture;
some dipped to the neck,
others soaping their complexions
in the midst of Nature's pride
pictured in snow-capped mountains,
green glorious wilderness,
and here,
crystal-clear water:
yes, a moving picture of transition.

N. S. Sigogo

Born in the Filabusi district of Rhodesia in 1932. Educated at Malole and Shamba Schools and at Wanezi Mission School. Married and has five children. Has been employed as a teacher and a clerk, but recently joined the editorial staff of a Mission Press in Gwelo. Is interested in the development of vernacular literature in Rhodesia, with particular attention to the Ndebele language. His poems have appeared in various magazines and anthologies, and many of them have been broadcast in Rhodesia. Two novels: *Usethi Ebukhweni Bakhe* (Purnell, South Africa) and *Gudlindlu Mntanami* (Mambo Press, Rhodesia).

Tell Me The Reason

When we met in the woods,
You whispered a great tune;
Promising to die by my side.
But now you've parted away,
Laying my soul in a cold tomb,
NoNtando, tell me why.

Tell me why, NoNtando,
When we sat on a flat rock
Near the green grasses
Under a cold big shade,
You deceived me that way
And made me stay unfed.

Our maids make fires on hearths,
But you built yours in my heart;
For you believe mine is so large
That it be food of white ants
In the bush of abandonment.
NoNtando, why do you pain me so?

Even if I am lying alone in the veld,
Surfeited with the honey of bees,
When your name comes I hunger.
For you stole my soul away,
And left me an empty pail—
Howling like a lost dog.

You are a hard witch
Who cast evil spells on me
And made me ill undiseased.
I am now dwelling by the graves,
Waiting for someone to bury me
While I cry: Why do you make me cry?

Yea, you have forsaken me!
I'd better put on my sandals
And go to far-off lands,
Where no bird sings your name.
But before I leave tell me:
Why did you rend my heart?

Femi Sisay

Born in Freetown, Sierra Leone, in 1933, Femi Sisay (Mrs Delphine King Sisay) was educated at St George's Cathedral Primary School and the Freetown Secondary School for Girls. She has worked as a journalist and broadcaster in Nigeria for a number of years, and acted as interpreter and P.R.O. at the African Foreign Ministers' Conference and the African Heads of State Conference, both held in Lagos in 1962. She has travelled widely in Africa, Europe, the Middle East and the USA, and is at present in the USA where she teaches at a private college, whilst freelancing as writer, editor and lecturer. She has published one collection of poems, *Dreams of Twilight*, for which Chinua Achebe wrote the foreword.

Yon Pastures Green

Who knows
What disillusionments await,
What sweetness now will then turn sour
Before the open gate?
Who knows
What tragedies abide
The moment to unfold?
Then, weary traveller plodding on,
Discount not foolishly the present scene
In idle dream of yonder pastures green,
But rather savour well all that there is
That better, sweeter, still may seem
The fruits at journey's end.

African Drums

The drums roll out
Their old and solid song
Into my heart,
Into my innermost heart;

Songs as old as time,
As old as my people.
Stirred by this rhythm,
The body moves in unison
To the call of my ancestors
From times of yore,
Through the years and eons of time,
Through the eternal music of the drum,
Through the spirit that pervades
Our lives and theirs, too.

The drum, the silent union,
Silent as a desert,
Silent yet and strong
As the elephant,
That binds today to yesterday,
Bridges the years that span
Their time and mine,
Uniting us as one;
Roll out your rhythms magical,
Old drum symbol of Africa,
That jumped the thick rich forests
Peopled by trees' gigantic growths,
That crossed great rivers
Not crossable,
Glided over rocks—
Swift-flowing currents did not hinder you—
Faithful to your call, breaking the distance
Barrier, transmitting sounds,
Meaningful sounds
In answer to your call.

And yet your task's not ended,
Nor ever will you sing
From boxes solid and firm,
Rhythms liquid
Bathing my people,
My ancestors and those of my own time,
In joy, rejoicing gaily
As supple bodies ebony
Schooled from earliest youth—
Nay, from before the womb—

Sensitive to your sounds
They move, mingling their bodies
With your sounds
In one harmonious effort grand.

Roll out your rhythms,
Drum solid and firm,
Rhythms melodiously liquid,
Drum symbol of Africa,
Bearing within your secret depths
The power magical
To stir this native soul,
This soul within here lodged,
The soul in you, in me,
In all our ancestors,
That live on from before all time
Toward the consummation of all time,
The grand finale of all things.

Roll out your rhythms;
Call out to Africa her sons,
Call out to Africa her daughters,

And those within whom still may dwell
The soul of Africa undoubtedly will heed.

Wole Soyinka

Born of Yoruba parentage in 1935 at Abeokuta in Western Nigeria, Wole Soyinka is an actor, musician, and producer, as well as one of the most talented of the African poets and playwrights. He was educated at Ibadan University and at Leeds University, where he took an English Honours degree. After leaving Leeds he was attached to the Royal Court Theatre, London, where his play, *The Invention*, was staged. In 1960 he returned to Nigeria, where his play, *A Dance of the Forests*, won the *Observer* competition. His courage and outspokenness are legendary and already a myth has developed around his name. In 1967 he was imprisoned in Nigeria for his activities during the Civil War, and two of his poems were smuggled out of prison to be published as a leaflet by Rex Collings under the title *Poems from Prison* in 1969. He is at present Director of the School of Drama at the University of Ibadan. He has contributed to a wide range of magazines and anthologies, and his poetry has been translated into many languages. His publications include: *Three Plays* (Mbari, 1962), *The Lion and the Jewel*, play (O.U.P., 1963), *The Dance of the Forests*, play (O.U.P., 1963), *Five Plays* (O.U.P., 1964), *The Road*, play (O.U.P., 1965), *The Interpreters*, novel (Deutsch, 1966), *Idanre*, poems (Methuen, 1967) and *Kongi's Harvest*, play (O.U.P., 1968). The last of these plays has now been made into a film.

Purgatory

(An extract from *Bearings*)

Wall of flagellation to the South
Strokes of justice slice a festive air—
It is the day of reckoning.

In puppet cast: first, by law compelled
The surgeon, bottle primed for the ordeal;

Next, a cardboard row of gaolers, eyelids
Of glue—the observation squad. And—
Hero of the piece—a towering shade across
The prostrate villain cuts a trial swathe
In air, nostalgic for the thumbscrew,
Rack, and nail extractors—Alas,
All good things shall pass away—he adapts
To the regulation cane. Stage props:
Bench for a naked body, crusted towel,
Pail of antiseptic yellow to impart
Wet timbres to dry measures of the Law.

    The circus comes to circus town
    A freak show comes to freaks
    An ancient pageant to divert
    Archetypes of Purgatorio

For here the mad commingle with the damned:
Epileptics, seers and visionaries,
Addicts of unknown addictions, soulmates
To the vegetable soul and grey
Companions to the ghosts of landmarks
Trudging the lifelong road to a dread
Judicial sentence.

And some have walked to the edge of the valley
Of the shadow, and, at a faint stir in memories
Long faded to the moment of the miracle of reprieve
To a knowledge of rebirth and a promise of tomorrows
And tomorrows, and an ever beginning of tomorrows
The mind retracts behind a calloused shelter
Of walls, self-censor on the freedom of remembrance
Tempering visions to opaque masonry, to rings
Of iron spikes, a peace of refuge, passionless
And the comfort of a gelded sanity.

Weaned from the moment of death, the miracle
Dulled, his mind dissolves in shadows, a look
Empty as all thoughts are featureless which
Plunge to that lone abyss—And
Had it there ended? Had it all there ended
Even in the valley of the shadow of Night?

B. Tejani

Born 'on the slopes of Kilimanjaro' in 1942, B. Tejani studied Literature and Philosophy at Makerere University College, Kampala, before going on to Cambridge. He has contributed to *Cambridge Review*, *Zuka*, *Ghala* and *Sunday Nation* (East Africa) and was represented in *New Voices of the Commonwealth* (Evans). One of his plays and a short story have been broadcast by the BBC.

Wild Horse of Serengeti

With savannahs on our left
and on our right
the white-ribbed road
stretching to the sky,
we felt masters
of those alluvial plains
untrodden by man.

The car's boom
was our lonely space-flight,
its forward-thrusting power
our stream line,
its dust-storm
our rocket fuel.

When suddenly, with a jolt,
we came back to earth
as he stood
translucent,
sun-muscle coated,
with an arched neck
and thick nostrils
quicksilver quivering,
that wild horse of Serengeti.

K*

This was his kingdom,
the arid peace of the plains his,
the merged mountain and sky
and white-ribbed road,
where he stood square
with gunpowder feet.

At howl of machine-toot
lonely as a space-walk,
he exploded convulsively,
feet, limbs and body
boosting each other
and rose
rose . . .
and, my God!
came straight at us,
his dark hooves
kniving the air,
the haunches and belly
fighting a fierce wild Medea

and sailed clean
over the manned machine,
grazing raucously with
a black claw
the top
that dented
to his supremacy.

Larweh Therson-Cofie

A Ga-Adangbe, Larweh Therson-Cofie was born in Suhum, Ghana, in September 1943 and had his elementary education in Lagos, Nigeria. Returned to Ghana to further his education and later attended the Ghana Institute of Journalism in Accra. Some of his poems have been broadcast by the Ghana Broadcasting Corporation and others have appeared in *Okyeame*, Ghana's literary magazine. He lives in Ghana and works as a news reporter on the *Daily Graphic*.

Volta in Chains

Here lies the Volta
Trapped, caged, tamed,
Sprawling, sleeping
In this cage
Of steel
And rock
And concrete,
Whose colossal gates
Six sentinels
Guard day and night.

Here,
Here lies the Volta
Subdued, humbled,
Snoring
In this cage
Of steel
And rock
And concrete
Whose colossal gates
Six sentinels
Guard day and night.

Volta, Oh Volta,
Proud Volta,
Great Volta,
Where lies your might?
Where your valour?
Ungrateful man
Has enslaved you
At last?

Volta,
Proud Volta,
I pity you.
You used to come to our kitchen at night
And carried our ladles, cooking-pots and fowl away
Yet I pity you, Volta.
You used to stalk
Into our farms uninvited
And rooted our cocoyam and cassava away
Yet I pity you, Volta.
You used to raid our village unprovoked
And left our huts sprawling at your heels,
Yet I pity you, Volta,
I pity you—

In a like contraption
Guarded by five sentinels,
I also lie.

Ken Tsaro-Wiwa

Born at Bori in the Rivers State of Nigeria in 1941, Ken Tsaro-Wiwa was educated at Government College, Umuahia, and read English at the University of Ibadan where he played a very active part in both the Dramatic Society and the University Travelling Theatre. He was a postgraduate student in drama and has lectured at the University of Nigeria, Nsukka, and the University of Lagos. After the outbreak of the Civil War, he escaped from Nsukka, identified himself with the Federal Government and was appointed wartime administrator for Bonny in the Rivers State. He is currently Commissioner for Education in the Rivers State. He writes short stories, poems and plays.

Voices

They speak of taxes
Of oil and power

They speak of honour
And pride of tribe

They speak of war
Of bows and arrows

They speak of tanks
And putrid human flesh

I sing my love
for Maria.

For Her

From every coign of this loved room
Loved because we in it have lived
I see you soft as the twilight
That now caresses our soul
Uniting us in an eternity of love.

Darling, do you dream the dreams I dream
And do you walk the gardens of suave redolence
Through which I walk as I think of you?

And do you remember that day
When the dying sun shot gold-tinted arms
And we swam the river from shore to shore?
Do you remember the words I said to you?

Swiftly, swiftly, my skein of time unrolls
When from the deep well of your being
I slake the thirst of my love.

Night Encounter

Coming up the stairs
Through the light drizzle
One dark night, I met him
One with the darkness.
I stopped for a moment,
Frighted, tense.

He laughed gently and I relaxed,
Happy to find
In spite of the gun
He was still a man.

It lit the dark
That gentle laugh
In the pith of night . . .

Deeper that night
The skies wept heavy tears
But I heard only the low laugh
Of the soldier on patrol duty,
The man who was about to die.

Edwin Waiyaki

Born in Kikuyu, Kenya, in 1942, Edwin Waiyaki was educated at Alliance High School and Strathmore College, and later at Besançon University and the Institut des Hautes Études D'Outre Mer in France. At Strathmore College he was Features Editor of *The Scroll*. His work has appeared in various East African magazines and he contributed to *Drum Beat* (East African Publishing House) edited by Lennard Okola.

The Rupture

I dropped religion at the age of twelve,
Squirming at the truth behind the story
Of the burning horned black host of hell
And of white angels draped in glory.

Although I was as yet too young to delve
Deep down the pool I knew I was a quarry,
And never again would I well at the bell
Or stand the wild hosannas and the flurry.

I saw no ground for calls to ape the twelve
While howling whips around me grew more gory;
I wished they fell on those bound by the spell
Into blindness towards those equipped to worry.

Rain Breaking on Roof Thatch

Rain breaking on roof thatch
Is opiate harbinger of harvest
Faintly bleeding
The heart of the same sorrow
As sight of lovers clinging
At farewell time . . .

And in the hut
The drowsy children
Dangle shaved heads
Around the steaming pot . . .

And the blood of the mother
Ripples to the soothing throb
Of water striking straw.

To those whom this rain-music
Lulls to sleep,
Calm dreams:
Perhaps at festival
Bare-breasted dancers loom
To exotic drums
And frenzied pleading
Of spasmodic flutes.

At start of day
Rays streaming
From the womb of heaven
Through cracks,
Peer at peaceful faces
And pounded paste—
Caking unkissed away—
On rounded cheeks.

And I would each day love this drone
Of music muffled
To drug me to sleep.

Rain falling
On iron sheet or brick
Rattles like grit
Prattling menaces . . .

A portly father tells
Of spurting guns and blood
To a blue-eyed mother
And a toddling trio.

And in the depth of night
A fat, sweating soldier
Firing from a trench,
Wakens to the yelling of a child
Frozen by the muzzle of a bully's toy.

And when at last light
Ushers dreamers back
To busy yesterday,
A trembling child
Is hiding in his sheets!

But I would from the outset
Loathe to feel
My tinglish nerves,
Unhinged by raucous rain,
Run riot against my bones.